Thunder Rolling

The Story of Chief Joseph

By Helen Markley Miller

Illustrated by ALBERT ORBAAN

G. P. Putnam's Sons   New York

CONTENTS

THUNDER ROLLING

The Story of Chief Joseph

Chief Joseph's Route

— indicate route
• Battle of Clearwater Co.
• Cottonwood Skirmish
• Salmon Canyon Battle

Wash.

Ore.

Wallowa

Snake R.

Idaho

Salmon R.

Clearwater Fk.

Montana

Big Hole Battle

Camas Meadows

Missouri

Yellowstone

Park

Yellowstone R.

Laurell Skirmish

Wyo.

Bearpaw Battle

Cow Island

1. A CHIEF IS BORN

CHIEF JOSEPH of the Nez Perce Indians loved freedom above all other gifts of men.

This Joseph, whose Indian name means Thunder-Rolling-in-the-Mountain, has become famous in American history as a military genius. But he was really a man of peace.

For thirty-three years he fought stubbornly for the right of his people to live peacefully on the lands that had belonged to his tribe since the dawn days. At first he fought the government of the United States with words of unfailing logic.

But when words failed and he was forced into a war he did not want, he fought bravely with guns and bullets. He led his people through one of the greatest military retreats in history, a retreat to keep from war. During that retreat across fifteen hundred miles of can-

9

yon, desert, and mountain wilderness, he and his associate chiefs fought only when they were overtaken and attacked. But time and time again they outwitted the best military minds of the United States Army.

And when the last and decisive battle was lost, Chief Joseph accepted defeat to save the shedding of his people's blood. With dignity and without bitterness he set himself then to the task of caring for his people in a hated captivity. Until the end of his long life he fought on with quiet words to win back freedom for his people in the tribal lands that were dear to them.

The boy who was to become Chief Joseph was born in 1840 in Wallowa, the Land of the Winding Waters, the summer camp of his people.

The white men have no record of the birth of this great leader who was to cause them so much trouble. The wagons of the first settlers had not yet rolled across the sagebrush plains of Idaho's Snake River. There were white missionaries on Nez Perce land to the north, at Lapwai near what is now Lewiston, Idaho. But the mission did not record the birth of Indian babies born outside its boundaries. What was one more Indian baby in the teepees?

However, Chief Joseph himself stated in 1878, "I was born in eastern Oregon thirty-eight winters ago."

His father, Hohaats Tuekakas, Oldest Grizzly Bear,

10

was the head chief of all the Lower Nez Perces, wealthi-
est band of the rich Nez Perce Nation. The Indians of
this nation had roamed for centuries over thousands of
square miles of high plateau land in what is now south-
ern Washington, eastern Oregon and central Idaho.

Oldest Grizzly Bear's band owned by ancient tribal
right all the land between Oregon's Blue Mountains to
the west and Idaho's Snake River to the east. It was an
area about the size of the state of Rhode Island. They
called their country the Land of the Winding Waters
because it was kept green by many clear streams.

In the winter they moved their vast herds of spotted
Appaloosa horses north to the warm and protected
valleys of the Imnaha and Grand Ronde Rivers. But
every summer they pitched their teepees beside the blue-
green waters of Wallowa Lake. It was there beneath
massive, snow-covered mountains that Chief Joseph
was born.

Oldest Grizzly Bear wanted a son who might be
chosen chief after him. Perhaps, while he awaited news
of the baby's arrival, he asked the Great Spirit Chief
of his fathers to give him a son. But it is more likely
that he prayed haltingly to the new God, the God of
the white men. For he had been one of the first to travel
to the Presbyterian mission at Lapwai, one of the first to
be baptized in the little log-cabin chapel. Mission records
state that he was given the Christian name of Joseph.

11

Mentioned also is his remarriage under the white man's law to his wife of many years. She was then given the Christian name of Aranoth.

When a son was born to him, Old Joseph had a happy heart. The small chief-to-be was given no name, for that was the tribal custom. He was called Son of Tuekakas, Son of Old Joseph.

Since all Nez Perce children were reared according to strict tribal custom, the baby was laced into a cradleboard so that his back would grow straight and strong, so that he would be tall. As he grew, he was taught to heed the quiet words of his parents, to endure without crying the small daily hurts, never to whine and complain over misfortunes.

When the boy was three years of age, the old chief moved a part of his band to Lapwai to be near the mission. There was another son in the family now, and the two small boys no doubt romped and tussled in the dust about the teepee as they learned to get about on unsteady fat legs.

On Sundays they sat with their parents in the great circle to hear the Reverend Henry Spalding talk about Jesus. Proud indeed was the elder son of Old Joseph when he was baptized a few years later.

"I have a Christian name now, my father," the boy said. "I like being called Joseph after you."

"A-aa, yes, my son, you have a Christian name. But

12

you must earn your Indian name. Not even the strong God of the white man can give you that name."

In the log schoolhouse of the Spalding Mission, the boy Joseph and his brother, now eight and seven years old, started to school. But they had little time to learn much of the white man's speech and wisdom. Trouble between white man and red soon put an end to their schooling.

One day a messenger came riding a spent horse to the old chief's lodge. The boy Joseph listened while the Nez Perce told of trouble at the Waiilatpu Mission, forty miles over the hills to the west.

"Our cousins, the Cayuse Indians, have killed fourteen white people at the mission," the messenger related. "White soldiers have come. Five of the ones who killed have been caught. They will hang."

"The others?" the boy heard his father ask.

"They have escaped away into the hills."

Waiilatpu Mission was near what is now Walla Walla, Washington. It had been built by Dr. Marcus Whitman and his beautiful wife Narcissa. Now both had fallen before the tomahawks of the Cayuse, and the white people of the West were angry and fearful.

Darkened by the troubles of the massacre, life at the Spalding Mission was changed for Young Joseph. The schoolhouse doors were barred. There was no more preaching in the great circle.

13

"Our white chief Spalding," the boy Joseph told his brother, "shows the white feather. He has run away. He is afraid our father and the other chiefs will kill him. But our father is friends with the white man. He would not harm the white chief."

The shadow of a cloud seemed to cover the mission for Young Joseph. And the shadow grew darker when white soldiers accused his father of hiding the Cayuse Indians who had escaped. The boy hung around the edges of the council meeting to hear what his father would have to say.

"We must ride to Waiilatpu," his father told the other chiefs. "We must ask the white men for a peace talk. We will prove that we had nothing to do with the murders. We have not hid the murderers."

The lad's heart must have been big with pride as he watched his father ride off at the head of two hundred and fifty picked warriors. Above the chief's head waved the American flag, and in his hand he held high the Gospel, written in Nez Perce.

A few days later the peace party rode back to Lapwai. Small Joseph probably only knew that his father had been successful. But history records the old chief's dignified defense of his people before the white judges.

"Now I show you my heart," he had said. "When I left home I took the Book in my hand and brought it with me. It was my Light. . . . I speak for my people. I

14

do not want my children engaged in this war. You speak of the murderers. I shall not meddle with them. I bow my head. This much I speak."

And now Young Joseph learned for the first time that there could be quarrels even among Nez Perces. The Mission Nez Perces did not like sharing their lands with the Lower Nez Perces. The chief, Thunder Eyes, quarreled with Oldest Grizzly Bear because the huge herds of the Wallowa Indians grazed on land belonging to the Mission Indians.

Oldest Grizzly Bear called all his own people together one morning and announced so that all might hear:

"We will go back to our home. There we will stay. This land is not the land of our people. We will go back to Wallowa. That is our home."

The boy Joseph was glad to hear these words, for he loved the summer camp of his people. Summers there had always been fun.

2. TRAINING TO LEAD

IN THE Land of the Winding Waters the youthful Joseph set about his training for chieftainship. There is no record of that training, but since all Nez Perce youths went through the same training, his must have followed the pattern.

"You will not be chosen chief," his father no doubt told the boy, "because you are the son of a chief. You must prove yourself worthy if you want our people to choose you for their chief."

"My father, I will try," Young Joseph promised.

And so he set about his training seriously. He knew that he must do his best to surpass the other growing lads. He entered with spirit into all the games, the wrestling, the foot races. He learned to swim in the cold mountain streams and lakes. Not always could he win, for there were other strong lads in the band. His brother, who was a natural athlete, often excelled. But Young Joseph never shirked effort.

Since he had been old enough to stride a horse, he had been riding. Now he learned to ride his horse at high speed over the rough hills. He learned to gallop in the furious charge of the sham battle. He learned to cling to the side of his mount as he rode around and around an imaginary foe, shooting arrows that would not miss in spite of the horse's speed. He learned to force his horse through the mad white waters of swift rivers, where the current might sweep both rider and mount to their deaths.

"My father," the boy proudly told Oldest Grizzly Bear, "my horse and I are now one."

"A-aa, my son. It is good."

Young Joseph knew that he must also master the arts and crafts of his tribe. And so he learned from his father how to splice the horns of the mountain sheep to make a Nez Perce bow. When the lad finished his first bow, it was three feet long, highly polished, strong and true.

"The bow is good," Oldest Grizzly Bear said.

Young Joseph learned to chip spearheads and arrow points from the hard black obsidian rock. He learned to fashion a war bonnet of brightly dyed eagle feathers, and to make a bear-claw necklace.

18

"When I have a few more winters," he no doubt told his brother proudly, "I shall wear a war bonnet in battle. And I shall meet Hohaats, the Great Grizzly. I will kill him and take his claws from him."

At night from the wise old men of his band Young Joseph learned the tribal dances and chants of his people, and the history and legends of his race.

"It was Itsiyayi the Coyote," the old men said, "who, when the world was young, slew a great monster that lived on the plain of Kamiah. From the body he made all the Indian tribes of the mountains. But it was from the heart's blood that he made the Nez Perce tribe, noblest of all the mountain Indians."

The old men told the boy that there were four main bands of Nez Perce Indians and that all were brothers. Although they lived in different places, they were a nation. There were the Upper Nez Perces who clustered their villages around the mission, and Young Joseph already knew about them. The Kamiah Nez Perces lived to the north on the Clearwater River and the plain of Kamiah. The Salmon River Nez Perces lived in wild country deep in the canyon of the Salmon to the east.

"And we are the Lower Nez Perces, who live here in the Valley of the Winding Waters," Young Joseph said proudly.

Many stories of Itsiyayi the Coyote the growing

19

Joseph heard and was to remember. It was Coyote the Crafty, Coyote the Clever who always won by his wits when strength failed.

"A-aa," the boy said to his brother, "it is well to be strong like Hohaats the Great Bear. But it is also good to be clever like Coyote. It is good to win over warrior enemies by crafty thinking."

A favorite story with Young Joseph was the tale of the coming of the first white men to Nez Perce land. Over the hills of Weippe near Kamiah, the tribal council ground of the Nez Perce Nation, the bearded white strangers had ridden from the east. The names of their leaders had been Lewis and Clark. Clark had hair as red as the flames from the lodge fire. With him was a huge Negro servant with a face from which the black would not scrub, although the Nez Perces tried. The Indians had welcomed the white men, fed and lodged them, and then helped them make canoes to continue on their way down the big rivers to the sea. The Nez Perces had agreed never to make war on the white man.

"This promise the Nez Perces have never broken," the old men said. "No white man can accuse us of bad faith and speak with a straight tongue."

Now that there was no white man's school to attend, Young Joseph learned by heart the laws of his people.

"You must keep these laws yourself," his father told

20

him, "or you cannot expect your people to obey them if you are chosen chief."

And so the boy learned the following laws and determined to live up to them all his life:

> *Treat all men as they treat you.*
> *It is a disgrace to tell a lie.*
> *It is shame for one man to take from another his property without paying for it.*
> *Never be the first to break a bargain.*
> *The Great Spirit Chief sees and hears everything; he never forgets. He will give to every man a spirit home according to his life on earth.*

By the time the young chief-to-be had reached his tenth summer, he was well versed in the history, skills, and beliefs of his tribe. It was time now, he knew, for him to earn his Indian name. He was not surprised when his father called him into the lodge one summer day.

"My son," Oldest Grizzly Bear said solemnly, "you have seen ten winters. The time has come when you must go alone to the mountains to find your *wyakin*, your guardian spirit. The spirit of the mountain will send your *wyakin* to you in the form of bird or beast or spirit power. Your *wyakin* will give you a name. Your *wyakin* will keep you from danger all the years of your life. This much I speak."

"A-aa, my father," the youth answered. "I am ready."

As a man, Chief Joseph never spoke of his ordeal to win a guardian spirit and a name. But since all Nez Perce children were required to go through this sacred vigil, the boy's nights alone on the mountain must have been something like the following story.

He knew what he had to do, for he had listened to the beliefs of his people. He would win a good name. He would not come skulking back to the lodges without name or guardian spirit as did some of the rabbit-hearted youths who had to go to the mountains again and again. He would stay boldly on the mountaintop until his guardian spirit came riding the wind to give him a name.

He shucked off his buckskin shirt and leggings. Clad only in moccasins and breechcloth, he took the trail to the loftiest mountain that rose above the valley. He sped along the shores of blue Wallowa Lake. He climbed up through the pine forests until he reached a rocky shoulder of the lonely peak. Below was the lake, the shadows of the mountains already darkening its waters.

He looked up to see Tipyahlahnah the Eagle loose his crooked claws from the crag and swoop screaming away. He listened and heard Hohaats the Great Bear grunt and crash off through the sparse underbrush. But

22

Training To Lead

Young Joseph was not afraid. Harm, he had been told, never came to a child who searched for his *wyakin*. Following the custom of his fathers, he piled for himself a bed of rocks and fir boughs. He had brought no food, for he must fast until his guardian spirit came to him in a vision. Stretching himself on his stony bed, he lay motionless, his gaze fixed on the sunset light that now reddened the crest of the snow peak above him. All the rest of the daylight hours and all through the moon-bright night he stared at the shadowy mountain wall.

The next day walked on slow feet toward a dark and threatening night. Would his *wyakin* never come? He fell at last into sleep so deep that it was like death itself, and dreams more real than sight came to him.

As the black night grayed into dawn, he awoke to storm. Lightning slashed the clouds. Thunder rolled and echoed in the mountains. Triumph filled his thoughts, for with the thunderclap he saw his *wyakin* filling the gray sky with grayer mist. He heard the name given him roll back from the mountain peaks in the thunder's voice as his *wyakin* vanished into the mists.

Weak from his fast and stiff from lying so long on the rocks, he staggered to his feet. But he was triumphant as he walked back to the village.

Thunder Rolling

"My father," he said proudly, "now I have a name. Now I have a *wyakin*."

"My son," Oldest Grizzly Bear said, "that is good."

Young Joseph told no one, not even his father, what form his attending spirit had taken. This secrecy was tribal custom. The name he had won also must remain untold. Not until two moons had passed and the time had come for the Spirit Dance could his secret become tribal property.

On that autumn night, in the leaping red light of a central fire, Young Joseph waited his turn to dance and to chant a song that would reveal his *wyakin* and the hard-earned name. His heart beat high as he glanced around the circle of his people. Would they approve his name? No other lad had won a name so proud.

His turn came. He stepped into the circle with boyish dignity. He began his dance with slow rhythmic motions that increased in strength and power as they told of the coming of the storm, the rolling of the thunder. With all his force he chanted the words of a song that held his name, weaving it into his chant in as many different ways as Nez Perce speech allowed. He sang:

"Hin-mah-too-yah-lat-kekt,
Thunder travels over the mountains;
From the mountains thunder rolls.
Loud crashes the thunder.
Down from the mountains the thunder falls.

24

Training To Lead

Thunder rolls across the waters
Down from the mountains.
Hin-mah-too-yah-lat-kekt!
Thunder-Rolling-in-the-Mountains!"

His song finished, he stood waiting with upflung arms for the approval of his people. He stood tall, feeling strength and assurance flood through all his body. His heart seemed to grow big with pride when he heard a whisper of acceptance swell to a loud murmur of approval.

"The son of our chief speaks good words," the people said to each other. "His *wyakin* is powerful. Who can harm the thunder? Who can crush the mountain? Hin-mah-too-yah-lat-kekt shall be his name. Thunder-Rolling-in-the-Mountains is his name. A-aa! It is good."

Young Joseph was very proud of his new Indian name, but he knew that he was still many years of training from chieftainship.

"It is woman's work to prepare and cook food," his father told him, "but it is the duty of a man to provide."

Young Joseph learned to track the deer through the fallen leaves or new snow, to bring down the swift antelope with his arrows, to spear the salmon that came leaping up the streams every summer to reach their birthplace and spawn. He joined in the general fall hunt that was to supply his band with meat for the winter months.

25

Thunder Rolling

Once he rode far to the east with his father and other hunters across the Lolo Trail. This was the ancient path of his people to the buffalo grounds in Montana, the land of the friendly Crow Indians. Heart beating fast, he joined in the hunt of the great shaggy beasts. The thrill of the chase was his, the fast galloping to ride down the buffalo, the thrust of the spear when the huge animals grew tired from the constant running.

Back over the Lolo Trail he rode, proud because he had helped to supply meat for his band and buffalo hides for protection from the winter cold. He almost wished the band had met with enemy Indians so that he could have had a chance to prove his skill in war. He could handle the white man's gun now, and shoot its murderous bullets straight. But he knew his father would not have let him fight until he was older.

During these years of Young Joseph's training, his younger brother went through the ordeal of the *wyakin* and won the name of Ollocot, the Frog.

Between the two boys there was deep brotherly love. Both were handsome, although very different in nature. Ollocot was always laughing, impulsive, courageous, and high-spirited. But Young Joseph was serious-minded. He never made a decision until he had thought out a problem carefully. But he was very sure that he was right once a decision had been reached.

Training To Lead

Years later he said, "I have carried a heavy burden on my shoulders since I was a boy."

That burden was the knowledge that he must fit himself for chieftainship. He knew that he must prepare himself for his high task by learning to think carefully and to decide right. Otherwise, he never would be able to make his people follow his lead. He had to have the sure pride, the quiet dignity, the force and power that make a man a leader.

3. FIRST TREATY

Young Joseph was fifteen years old when his
burden began to grow heavier. It was then that he saw
with his own eyes and heard with his own ears the
treachery of the white man.

No doubt before this he had been told by others
that the white man was a threat to the Indian way of
life. But Wallowa was well off the Oregon Trail, the
road of the westward-pushing settlers. The Land of
the Winding Waters was protected from chance settlement by the high Wallowa Mountains and by the deep
canyon of the Snake, now famous as Hell's Canyon.

From his cousins the Cayuses and from members of
visiting Nez Perce bands, Young Joseph now began to
hear angry growls against the settlers. The white men
were clearing land to the north and south, the east

29

and west. They were plowing fields, building cabins, and settling down to stay. Even Oldest Grizzly Bear, always friendly to the white man, grew worried.

"I see through the schemes of the white men," he told his son. "We must be careful in trading with them. They want too much to make money. They want land."

The white men were taking over all the country to the west as if it were their own land, Young Joseph learned. They had divided the land that spread west to the ocean, and they called their divisions territories. Oregon Territory, now that so many white people had settled there, had grown too large to rule easily. And so the white men had carved Washington Territory from it and had appointed a man called Isaac Stevens to be chief over it.

One day Young Joseph was with his father when a message came from Governor Stevens calling all the Indian chiefs of the mountain area to a great treaty council on the banks of the Walla Walla River.

"The Cayuse Indians will be there," Old Joseph told his son, "and the Umatilla, Palouse, and Yakima tribes. The head chiefs of the four Nez Perce bands are to come."

"What does the white chief want?" Young Joseph asked.

"I do not know. I am afraid they will try to take our lands."

First Treaty

"You will go, my father?"

"I will go. I am willing to talk things over with the white men. But they will not get our land."

The old chief was silent for a few minutes, his head bowed. Young Joseph waited respectfully. He loved his father and hated to see him worried. His father was tall and strong and wise. He had a will so like iron that all his people obeyed his word without question. He would never give up the Valley of the Winding Waters to the greedy white men.

"My son," Oldest Grizzly Bear said at last, "you have seen fifteen winters. You must now learn wisdom and self-control in council with the white men. When I am gone, you will need to know the strength of words. You will ride with me to the meeting place."

Young Joseph's heart beat fast with pride and eager anticipation but he answered quietly, "A-aa, my father. I will listen with sharp ears."

In the upper valley of the Walla Walla the four Nez Perce bands met to ride as a nation to the council. Young Joseph stayed close to his father at first, but soon he was mingling with the other youthful Indians who had come to watch.

There was much to see. He watched with eager curiosity while the gathered warriors prepared for their ceremonial entry. He helped the braves streak their bodies with white and slash bold yellow and

31

crimson paint across the white. He helped them decorate their horses' bridles with trinkets and braid eagle feathers into manes and tails. He admired the fierce, warlike appearance of the warriors. Soon, he thought, he too would be old enough to don the ceremonial paint.

When the cavalcade started for the council ground, he rode at first beside his father. Twenty-five hundred strong, the Nez Perce warriors of the four bands rode to the council ground, and Young Joseph knew a high pride in his people.

It was May in 1855. He saw the hawthorns blooming white along the river's edge and the sun shining on fields of spring flowers. But when he counted the many white tents of the soldiers set on the green meadow, there must have been a chill at his heart. The Stars and Stripes floating above the council tent spoke of the power of the white soldiers. His sharp eyes noticed that no teepees had been set up beside the river.

"My father," he said, "the Nez Perces are the first to come. And the soldiers are many."

"They are many. And we are few. Do not worry. The other tribes will come."

The chiefs gave the signal to approach with all ceremony. Young Joseph, regretful that he was not yet a warrior, drew his horse to one side. He sat straight in his saddle, his handsome face lighting with a fierce joy as he watched a thousand chosen warriors wheel swiftly to form a single line. Armed with shields, bows, lances, and guns, the braves paced their horses slowly nearer the soldiers' camp. Here they halted.

His father and the other chiefs rode forward to meet Governor Stevens. Young Joseph, his boy's heart athrill with excitement, watched with pride. At a signal the warriors came on, drums beating in time to the wild, wordless singing of a Nez Perce chant. In swift circles the braves rode around the governor and the chiefs, galloping up in mock charge and wheeling back to ride in the circle of Indian attack. All the time wild Indian shouts rose to the hills.

Twenty-five picked warriors flung themselves from their horses to form in a ring and dance for the white chiefs to the furious beating of tom-toms. Young Joseph felt his body tingle with desire to join the dancers. He knew that dance.

The dance over, the warriors withdrew to the meadow where the women already were setting up poles for teepees. The younger boys began herding the horses into the rye grass.

Young Joseph did not join the youths. He had come to learn the ways of white man and red in council. Now he would learn. He slipped from his horse, slapped its rump to send it off with the herd, and went to stand behind his father. Oldest Grizzly Bear was smoking a

33

pipe of peace with the white chiefs. He smiled briefly at his son, and the boy knew that he had been right to come.

Six days later, when all the Indian tribes were assembled, Young Joseph stood again behind his father while Governor Stevens made known through an interpreter the purpose of the council.

"The Great White Father in Washington," the governor said, "wants to prevent war between white man and red. He knows that unless land is set aside for the use of the Indians, the settlers will take what land they choose. The Indians will fight this taking of their lands. Blood will spill. War will come on quickly."

Young Joseph thought the white chief was speaking with a straight tongue. Perhaps the white men were going to be fair in this council. If their law said that no white man could settle in Wallowa, then his father's people could live there peacefully forever.

But the white chief was not through talking. He was saying that the United States was willing to buy lands for the settlers from the Indians. The government would pay $650,000 for certain lands owned by the various tribes. The money would be paid in yearly installments.

Young Joseph felt a gnawing sickness of fear when he heard the governor tell what lands the white men wanted to buy for themselves. Part of Wallowa was

34

included in the lands to be sold to the United States.

He did not want his father to sell any of the Land of the Winding Waters. Why should the Indians sell what was theirs just to keep the white men from taking land that did not belong to them? What good would all that money be to the Indians if there were no grasslands left for their herds?

"Three generous reservations of land will be set aside for the Indians: one for the Walla Walla, Cayuse, and Umatilla tribes; one for the Yakimas, and one for the Nez Perces," the governor said. "No white man will be allowed to settle on these reservations forever."

Young Joseph was bewildered. Why should the Nez Perces live confined within a few miles when this whole land was theirs to roam by ancient right?

"This treaty will give to the Indians," the governor was saying now, "all hunting, fishing and grazing rights on any land outside the reservation—any land unclaimed by white settlers."

There was something wrong with this promise too, Young Joseph decided. The white settlers would soon want all the land. They would leave no grazing valleys unclaimed.

"We will give you training in mechanics, teachers and schools, sawmills and gristmills and shops," the governor was promising.

Young Joseph grew more puzzled. What would his

35

people do with machines? What did they want of shops and mills?

Young Joseph's bewilderment increased. And now he was angry. If this was the way of the white men in council, the boy thought, then their way was wrong. They were planning to take land from the Indians and make that taking look as if it were a kindness. This was a double-faced treaty.

The chiefs also were bewildered and angry. They murmured among themselves. Governor Stevens dismissed the council to let the chiefs think the treaty over.

Eleven days of talk followed before any of the chiefs would sign the treaty. Then, not understanding what they were doing, they began putting their marks down on the governor's paper.

Young Joseph watched Oldest Grizzly Bear with fear. Would his father sign away the lands of his people, those loved valleys and mountains of Wallowa? The boy had a shaking heart, but the next moment he knew relief and a fierce pride in his father. The old chief put his finger on that part of the map that marked Wallowa.

"I will not sign any paper that does not show all this land as mine," he said firmly. "I have no other home than this. I will not give it up to any man."

36

First Treaty

Young Joseph knew that his father meant what he had said. Now what would the white chief do?

Governor Stevens studied the stern old face before him and then drew a new line on the map. The boy saw that the line now ran from the top of the Blue Mountains to the canyon of the Snake. It took in all the lands that belonged to his father's people.

"A-aa, now it is good," Oldest Grizzly Bear said. And he put his mark on the paper.

Proud of his father, Young Joseph rode back with him to the Valley of the Winding Waters, which had been saved a little longer for their people.

The boy was jubilant, but the old man said: "Do not fool yourself, my son. The white man grows strong in the land. Soon he will come to us again and say, 'We want your land.'"

Young Joseph rode in silence for a time, and then he said, "My father, I have learned two things at the white man's council. One is that the white man will take what he can get."

"And the other lesson, my son?"

"That wise words, firm words, will sometimes defeat the white man."

37

4. THE LIE TREATY

AFTER the treaty of 1855 had been signed, there was peace for a time. Then the tribes who had sold land began to understand what they had done. Dissatisfied with the treaty and unhappy because even reservation land was overrun by the whites, many of the tribes went on the warpath.

"Will we go to war too?" Young Joseph asked his father.

"No, my son. Many years ago we gave our word not to fight the white man. We will keep that promise. And we have our land. Why should we fight?"

The rebelling tribes were defeated by 1858, and the treaty was enforced. The white men took the land they had bought, but the government did not pay the Indians until two years later. Oldest Grizzly Bear then received his share.

"Will we keep the money?" Young Joseph asked.

"I am telling you, No. We do not want their money. We have not sold them any land. If we take the money, they will say that we took pay for our country, and that it is theirs. I have never sold our land."

Young Joseph, with all the others of his band, realized the wisdom of the old chief's decision. But the other Nez Perce bands joyfully took their payments. Their joy did not last long. The first payment was their last for many years. The Civil War had begun, and the government needed all its money. To make matters worse, the white men did not stay off the reservation lands set aside for the Indians.

Young Joseph heard that a man named Pierce with a party of prospectors seeking gold had ridden deep into the Nez Perce Reservation near the opening of the Lolo Trail. He had filled his gold pan, swirled it, and found the yield good. From that moment the terms of the treaty were broken again and again.

"The white men are too greedy for gold," Young Joseph said.

The following winter he visited the mission at Lapwai with some of his band. He had upsetting news to tell his father when the band returned.

"My father, the white men make trouble for our

brothers at the mission. There are many white men at
the mouth of the Clearwater. They have built a store
there to sell supplies and tools to the men who dig for
gold. Now there is a big village of white people there.
They call the village Lewiston."

"A-aa, the white man grows too strong."

"They claim land that belongs to Nez Perces. I saw
white men tear down Indian fences and use the logs
to fence their own fields. I saw them turn their cattle
in to graze on Nez Perce corn. The white men even
murder Nez Perces."

"Are they punished?"

"The white man's law does not punish white men,"
Young Joseph said bitterly.

A few years later when he was with his people at
their summer camp in Wallowa, a message came for
his father to attend another council.

Oldest Grizzly Bear sighed. "There will be more
treaty talk. You will go with me. Ollocot also will go."

A man grown now, Young Joseph was wiser than
he had been about the first council.

"What good will come of more treaty talk?" he
asked his father. "The white men have not kept the
promises of the first treaty."

The old chief shook his head sadly. "They have a
plan. They will ask the Nez Perces to give up more
of their land to the White Fathers in Washington."

"How much land?"

"Ten thousand square miles. That is what the message says. The white men will cut the Nez Perce Reservation to six hundred square miles."

"The Valley of the Winding Waters? They will take our land this time?" Young Joseph asked with fear.

"They will try. They want White Bird's land also. He will not give up his Salmon River hills."

"And we will not give up Wallowa," Young Joseph said angrily.

With a sick heart Young Joseph rode with his father and Ollocot to the council at Lapwai. All the Nez Perce chieftains were there. Fierce old White Bird was there to fight for his hills. Big Thunder, head chief of the Mission Indians, was in favor of the treaty because none of his boundaries were to be changed. There were two chiefs from Kamiah: Eagle-from-the-Light, who wanted nothing to do with a new treaty, and Chief Lawyer, who thought the treaty would be a fine thing for his people. Lawyer had won his name because he was a great talker.

The gathered Indians saw nothing wrong when the white men appointed Chief Lawyer to talk for all the Nez Perce bands. In the council he seemed quite willing to listen to what the white men had to say.

"And why should he not listen willingly?" Young Joseph said to Ollocot. "Lawyer's village, Kamiah, will not be touched. The white chiefs say they are going to make him head chief over all the bands."

Ollocot smiled, but there was bitterness in the smile. "The head chief will be paid five hundred dollars a year."

"Chief Lawyer is crafty. He is like Itsiyayi the Coyote," Young Joseph said.

He was glad when his father, White Bird, and Eagle-from-the-Light refused to have anything to do with the treaty.

"I will not sign your paper," Oldest Grizzly Bear said. "I am no child. I can think for myself. I have no other home than Wallowa. I will not give it up to any man. My people would have no home. Take away your paper. I will not touch it with my hand."

For weary days the council on the mission grounds dragged on. Finally those chiefs who would not sign grew tired of the talk and withdrew from the council.

That night at one of the lodges, Young Joseph sat near his father and listened to fifty-three chiefs and warriors of the Nez Perce Nation talk the treaty over. The sun rose. Still the chiefs could not agree as a nation to the terms of the treaty. Oldest Grizzly Bear, Eagle-from-the-Light, and White Bird rose from the council fire.

"Our hearts and your hearts are like shaking hands," they told Chief Lawyer. "We are brothers. But we cannot sell our homes to the white men. From this sun forth, we will not act as one. You and Big Thunder do what you want about the treaty for your people. We will not give up our lands."

Young Joseph bowed his head in grief when he heard these words. He knew that this was the last council fire of one of the greatest Indian nations west of the Rockies. The Nez Perces would lose their strength when they no longer acted as one tribe.

Chief Lawyer hastily signed the treaty for his own village. Big Thunder also signed. Without knowing it, Chief Lawyer had sold out his brothers. The white men at once declared that Lawyer, as head chief for all the Nez Perce bands, had signed for all. The treaty, said the white men, was now binding on all four bands.

Young Joseph could not believe when he heard that the Salmon River Country and Wallowa now belonged to the United States.

He stood with his father in the door of their lodge when word was brought to the old chief.

"That thief treaty!" Young Joseph said, his grief choking him, burning like a fire in his throat. "That lie treaty! Our land is gone. Wallowa is gone."

Oldest Grizzly Bear tore up his copy of the treaty in a mighty wrath. He destroyed his beloved New Testament, the Nez Perce's Book of Heaven.

"From this day," he made solemn promise, "I will

44

have nothing to do with the white men, nor with the white man's ways."

Back to Wallowa with his sons rode Oldest Grizzly Bear to live out the remainder of his days in quiet dignity and in complete disregard of the terms of that treaty of 1863.

The old chief ordered Young Joseph and the other men to set out boundary stakes around the thousand hills and valleys of Wallowa so that his people would understand how much land they owned by tribal right.

"Inside is the home of our people," he proclaimed so that all might hear. "The white men may take the land outside. Inside this boundary all our people were born. It circles the graves of our fathers, and we will never give up those graves to any man."

Young Joseph made a solemn vow to himself. When he became chief, he would do all in his power to keep the land inside those stakes for his people.

5. NEZ PERCE BRIDE

YOUNG JOSEPH was now twenty-four years old. He was man-grown, he told himself. He stood six feet two inches in his moccasins. The foot races, the swimming, the games, the horseback contests, had given him broad shoulders, strong muscles, a big chest. He knew that he had dignity and a strength that needed no boasting words to make itself felt. He regretted that he never had been tried in battle so that he could be a war chief, but he knew with pride that he was accepted as a brave and forceful leader by the men of his band.

Now it was time for him to choose a wife, he decided. At the last council in Lapwai he had seen a laughing maiden, sweet and comely. She was warm like the lodge fire of a winter night, kind as the mountain breeze in the hot days of summer. She was daughter to Chief

Whistasket of Lapwai. Toma Alwawinmy she was called, Driven-Before-a-Cold-Storm. Young Joseph knew that he wanted this maiden for his bride.

Although Chief Joseph never told the story of his own courtship and marriage, both must have been accomplished according to the fixed tribal customs of the Nez Perces.

The young brave rode his sleekest horse to Lapwai. He knew better than to approach the girl at once with his offer of marriage, for Nez Perce maidens were guarded well by their parents. There would be no permitted meetings under the alders by the creek in Tsemenicum, Friendly Land of Warmth and Sunshine. But he hoped that if he took part in the races and contests of the village youths, his maiden would notice his ease at the horseback riding, his skill with spear and bow and arrow.

At night he stood in the shadows outside her teepee. While the moon silvered the alders and touched the hills with friendly light, he played his flute, letting it tell her in music of his love.

Toma Alwawinmy watched and listened, and she found this handsome brave from the band beyond the hills to her liking. At the games she admired Young Joseph. She saw that his chin was square, his black eyes dark and piercing, his mouth sweet, yet firm and strong. She liked his glossy black hair with his scalp

48

lock cut long in front to give him even more height, and the side hair braided after the manner of her tribe. She liked the single eagle feather that he wore thrust through the back hair. She even liked his flute playing.

Slipping from her father's lodge in the dark, she met him secretly in the shadow of the trees lining the stream that the Mission Indians called Laaps, the Place of the Butterflies. There Young Joseph asked her to become his bride, and she accepted.

The first step was over, Young Joseph told himself happily. Now he must go to the lodge of Chief Whistasket to ask for the hand of Toma Alwawinmy. This he could do without the aid of his parents because he was the son of a chief and would be a welcome suitor. Chief Whistasket smiled and did not seem surprised. The old chief no doubt had been kept awake by the nightly serenades.

"What have you to give my daughter?" he asked shrewdly.

"A lodge in the Land of the Winding Waters," Young Joseph answered, his heart shaking for fear it might not be enough. "Fat cattle and many horses. Plenty buffalo skins for beds. Plenty deer meat and salmon for the winter cold. Plenty of everything."

"And you, my son? Tell me of yourself," Whistasket demanded, smiling because he already knew the answer.

49

"My father is Hohaats Tuekakas, chief of the Wallowa band of Nez Perces. I hope to be chief after him."

"You are prepared to be a chief, my son?"

"I have trained myself for many years. I am ready. My father grows old. I fear it will not be long before I must lead my people."

"And your people? Will they choose you for their chief?"

Young Joseph smiled his assurance. "In their minds they think of me already as chief."

"My son, it is good. In one moon the girl shall be yours."

Young Joseph rode back to Wallowa with a happy heart. His only unhappiness was that he could not see his maiden again until she rode to his lodge to become his bride. This separation was Nez Perce custom.

Toma Alwawinmy spent the month before her marriage in making the soft doeskin robe dictated by tribal custom for a Nez Perce maiden's wedding dress. Made of beautifully tanned skins whitened with clay, the garment reached to her ankles. She sewed long white doeskin fringes over every seam of the robe. She beaded the back and front with intricate patterns worked in bright blue and yellow beads and in porcupine quills dyed red, blue, and green. Beaded doeskin leggings she made, and soft, pliable moccasins. She cut a strip of white rabbit fur to bind in her black

braids, and made a purple silken band to wind about
her head.

One month after her betrothal day Toma Alwawinmy donned the finished robe. Watching with eager
eyes from her teepee, she saw a band of women, gay
in festive robes, riding to her lodge door. It was the
women of Young Joseph's family—his mother Aranoth, his sister Sarah, with other relatives. The women
were riding to fetch the maiden to her new home.

"Come," the bride called to her mother. "They are
here."

Toma Alwawinmy and her mother met Young
Joseph's mother at the door of the lodge.

"We come to give you welcome into our family,"
Aranoth said, smiling her pleasure at the girl who
waited, shy and lovely. "We are happy to see you. Will
you come with us to your home?"

"I will come. My heart says to go with you," Toma
Alwawinmy replied.

The women of Young Joseph's family rested that
night in the lodge of Whistasket. The next morning
the bride rode with them back to the Valley of the
Winding Waters. Here a great wedding feast had been
prepared. Toma Alwawinmy and Young Joseph sat at
the head of the feast. He was proud of his soft-eyed
bride and distributed presents to the guests with a
lavish hand. In return she took from the hands of each

friend the horn spoon used as eating utensil during the feast. A month later Young Joseph rode with his bride and all his family to Lapwai, where the feasting was repeated with the bride's family.

The tribal marriage was over. Young Joseph and Toma Alwawinmy rode back to the lodge made for them in the Valley of the Winding Waters.

For seven years Young Joseph lived with his band at peace in Wallowa. He helped his aging father with the ruling of the people, listening to his words of wisdom. As Oldest Grizzly Bear grew blind and feeble, he leaned more and more on his stalwart elder son. Gradually Young Joseph assumed the duties of a chief as his father grew too weak to rule.

These duties were not easy for the young man. There was bad blood between the reservation Indians and his own people. The Nez Perces around the mission who were living under the rule of the Indian agent at the reservation now called the Wallowa and the Salmon River Nez Perces the "Non-treaty Indians," making the term one of contempt. The Wallowa Nez Perces responded by ridiculing the farms of the Mission Indians and relating the joys of their free life—hunting and fishing, and herding their horses. Young Joseph had to prevent many quarrels from turning into bloodshed.

White settlers, scornful of the stakes that Old Joseph had set out about his lands, moved in to squat on claims in Wallowa. There were disputes about the ownership of horses and cattle, quarrels about fences. All these Young Joseph had to settle.

But hardest of all to meet were the demands that the Non-treaty Indians leave their home and come to the reservation to live. The Indian agent kept at the old chief and his son until Young Joseph grew tired of the argument.

"He is like a horsefly tormenting us," he told his father.

"We must brush off the horsefly," the old man said.

To all demands both the old chief and Young Joseph refused to listen.

"No," Young Joseph said briefly, talking for his father. "This is our home. Here we will stay."

When the agent threatened not to send the yearly payment, Young Joseph smiled. "We have never taken any of the payments. We have not sold you anything. We do not need your money. When we need money, all we have to do is sell some of our horses."

When the agent offered gifts of money or supplies, Young Joseph refused them.

"We do not need anything from you," he said. "We have our land."

One day Oldest Grizzly Bear sent for his son. With a sad heart Young Joseph saw that his father was dying. He took the trembling hand of the aged chief in his own

53

strong clasp and bent his head to listen to the last words of wisdom.

"My son," Oldest Grizzly Bear said, "my body is returning to my Mother Earth, and my spirit is going very soon to the Great Spirit Chief. When I am gone, think of your country. You will be the chief of these people. They look to you to guide them. Always remember your father never sold his country. You must stop your ears whenever you are asked to sign a treaty selling your home. A few more years, and the white men will be all around you. They have their eyes on this land. My son, never sell the bones of your father and mother."

"I will protect your grave with my life," Young Joseph promised, knowing in his heart that the task would be a severe one.

His father smiled. That night he went away to the Spirit Land. In the dawn a warrior paced a black horse slowly through the village.

"Now Oldest Grizzly Bear sleeps," he proclaimed. "Hohaats Tuekakas sleeps."

Young Joseph's heart wept, although he managed to keep unmanly tears from his eyes. His strong, wise father was gone. The chief's high task, the task of keeping Wallowa from the white men, now rested on the shoulders of the son.

54

6. BATTLE OF WORDS

Joseph was at once elected head chief over his father's people. He was not surprised, since for many years he had been virtual chief. But he was gratified. And he was concerned, for troubles with the white men were growing.

Almost immediately after he became chief a hundred settlers moved into the Wallowa Valley. Legally the white men had rights because the land had been thrown open to settlement by the United States Government. But Chief Joseph complained to the settlers.

"You take all the best pasture land," he said. "You build fences that keep our stock from grazing. You use up the water from our streams."

The settlers laughed. "If you want to argue about the land, do your arguing with the United States."

55

Chief Joseph now began his long battle of words that was to last for many years. A new Indian agent, John Montieth, had been appointed at Lapwai. Chief Joseph met with the agent in Wallowa to talk matters over.

"By the treaty of 1855," Montieth said, "your people kept most of Wallowa. But in 1863 the Nez Perces sold their land."

"My father never sold this country," Joseph argued. "He did not sign the lie treaty. We have never taken any money for this land. Wallowa is still ours."

Agent Montieth was fair. He investigated the valley and decided that the land around Wallowa Lake was too high for anybody but the Indians, too cold for anything but stock raising. He sent a report of his findings to President Ulysses S. Grant. The President set aside a large part of the Wallowa Valley for the Nez Perces and decreed it closed to any more white settlement.

Chief Joseph had won this battle, but he was not satisfied. The new boundaries took much of the tribal land from his band.

Six years of quarreling with the agency officials and the government followed. Chief Joseph now became a diplomat. He rode to councils when he was requested to do so. At the councils he spoke with perfect dignity and reasonableness. Always he talked through an interpreter. Although he understood English, he knew that he could best express himself in his own speech.

When he was told that he must come upon the reservation for the Nez Perces, he replied: "I will not. The reservation is too small for so many people with all their stock. We are free now. We can go where we please. Our fathers were born here, here they died, here are their graves. We will never leave them."

When he was told that he was bound by the treaty of 1863, he answered: "If we ever owned the land we own it still, for we never sold it. . . . Suppose a white man should come to me and say, 'Joseph, I like your horses, and I want to buy them.' I say to him, 'No, my horses suit me. I will not sell them.' Then he goes to my neighbor and says to him, 'Joseph has some good horses. I want to buy them but he refuses to sell.' My neighbor answers, 'Pay me the money, and I will sell you Joseph's horses.' The white man then returns to me and says, 'Joseph, I have bought your horses and you must let me have them.' If we sold our lands to the government, this is the way they were bought."

In 1875 Chief Joseph learned that President Grant had taken back the order closing Wallowa and had re-opened the country to settlers.

"The Great White Father in Washington speaks with a forked tongue," Joseph said angrily. To a Nez Perce the breaking of a promise was a sin.

That same year Chief Joseph met for the first time the United States general who was to become his bitter enemy. General Oliver O. Howard, the new Commandant of the Department of the Columbia, was visiting the Umatilla Reservation in eastern Oregon when Chief Joseph also arrived for a visit.

"I would like to meet the new war chief of the white men," Chief Joseph said.

General Howard wrote of that meeting:

> Joseph put his large black eyes on my face, and maintained a fixed look for some time. It did not appear an audacious stare; but I thought he was trying to open the windows of his heart to me, and at the same time endeavoring to read my disposition and character. . . . I think that Joseph and I became then quite good friends.

One day not long after this meeting two white men who had settled in the Wallowa Valley lost some horses. As usual, they blamed the Nez Perces and set out for the Indian village to find and reclaim their horses. Welotyah, a good and respected Nez Perce, objected to being accused of stealing. Unarmed, he tried to take a gun from one of the men. The other white man fired. Welotyah fell dead.

Chief Joseph was sad of heart. All the years of his chieftainship he had followed a twofold aim: to keep

58

the Wallowa for his people and to prevent bloodshed.

Now bloodshed had come—bloodshed that was deliberate murder. His fiery young men held an angry meeting and demanded revenge. He knew he must satisfy their demands, or more blood would spill. The duties of a chief were hard, he thought. He was the leader of his people, but he did not have the power to say yes or no. When his people talked around the council fire, it was his duty as chief to listen and to carry out the will of the greater number.

Again he rode to a council with the white men. He would do what he could. Perhaps, he thought, smiling to himself, this trouble could be turned into a means of keeping Wallowa for his people. Like Coyote, he would try craft. He would put the white people in the wrong. At the council he presented his case boldly.

"Welotyah was willfully murdered by the white men," Joseph said. "I now claim the land for the life taken. I shall hold the land for myself and for my people from this time forward, forever. All the whites must be removed from the valley."

His craftiness did not work. The two white men were tried by a jury of ranchers. The murderers were acquitted, as Chief Joseph had known they would be. Bad feeling flamed among the Indians. War threatened.

Finally the government, fearing that war would start, ordered Agent Montieth to place all the Non-treaty Nez Perces on the reservation by force. He was to have the aid of General Howard and all the United States troops at his disposal.

When Montieth's order reached Chief Joseph, he bowed his head for a long minute. Was Wallowa lost to his people? Were the Nez Perces to lose these hills and valleys that had been theirs to hunt and fish through untold years?

"I cannot believe that even the white men could be so unjust," he told his brother.

"Will we go on the reservation?" Ollocot asked.

Joseph lifted his head and his jaw set. "No. I am not through fighting with words. We will make one more effort. Ride to Lapwai and ask for a meeting with Montieth and General Howard. I will send word to all the Non-treaty chiefs. All will come."

In May of 1877, Chief Joseph rode with his fifty warriors to his last sad council at Lapwai. Courteously he greeted the one-armed General Howard. Keen Indian eyes took note of the general's erect, soldierly bearing, his broad shoulders, his quiet assurance.

Chief Joseph shivered slightly. He felt the cold storm wind of danger in the force and power gathered under the canopied council tent. Defeat for his people was in the stern eyes and hard handclasp of the blue-coated commander. The general had not come to the meeting to listen while Nez Perce chiefs spoke their hearts and showed their minds. He had come to give orders, and he intended to be obeyed. There was no friendship in Joseph's eyes now as he met those of the general.

"I heard that you wished to see me," Howard said coldly. "I am here to listen to what you have to say."

With quiet dignity Chief Joseph answered: "I will hear what you have to say to the chiefs. White Bird and his men are coming from the Salmon River Country. They will be here tomorrow."

"We will wait for White Bird," General Howard said sternly. "Instructions to him are the same as to you. You may as well know at the outset that you Indians must obey the orders of the United States."

Agent Montieth then read aloud the orders from Washington. They were what Chief Joseph had expected: all Non-treaty Nez Perces were commanded to leave their homes and move to the reservation.

Chief Joseph was silent. He was too sad, too hopeless to speak. Words of wisdom, he felt, would be useless at this council.

No more was said in that day's meeting, but that night there was talk about the campfire—long bewildered talk to which Joseph listened with a shaken heart.

The council began again in the morning. Chief Joseph sat on the bench among his friends. All the Non-treaty chiefs had not arrived, but the Nez Perces had chosen as their speaker the old chief of a small band that lived far to the south between the Salmon and the Snake. This Toohulhulzote was known as a fiery speaker.

Chief Joseph listened with a troubled mind while the general and Toohulhulzote held a small war of words. The excitable old chief was hotheaded and quarrelsome, the general cold and firm.

"Let the Indians take time," General Howard said at last, realizing that the talk was getting nowhere. "Let them wait until Monday morning. Meanwhile talk freely among yourselves."

Chief Joseph made every effort to hold back the rising wind of anger among his young hotbloods during that weekend. And he had reason to urge caution.

"A hundred soldiers have moved in," a rider from Wallowa brought word. "They are camped on the Grand Ronde near our winter home."

Joseph was worried. All of his warriors were with him. The women, the children, and the old men had been left unprotected. He called Ollocot to tell him the troubling news.

"A-aa," Ollocot said, "I have heard. I have heard that more soldiers are marching to Lapwai also."

Joseph sighed. "Soldiers all around us. General Howard is getting ready to show the Indians the rifle."

"One more time the white men lie to us," Ollocot said bitterly.

Battle of Words

"A-aa, we have come to a peace council, and peace talk should have no show of guns or force. But there are soldiers here with guns. Soldiers in our home country, too—with guns."

"What will we do?"

"Wait for the council on Monday. But keep the young men from talking war. You lead the young men. See that you keep them from bloodshed."

The chiefs of all the other Non-treaty bands had arrived for the final council. Joseph looked around at the gathered Indians. Looking Glass, now head chief of the Kamiah Indians, was a tall and powerful man of about forty years. His land was part of the reservation now, but his old chief, Eagle-from-the-Light, had not signed the treaty of 1863 when Lawyer did. Looking Glass considered himself a Non-treaty Indian. There was seventy-year-old White Bird, hiding his face with the eagle wing which was the sign that he was a medicine man. Old Toohulhulzote was ready with his thick, guttural speech, his tongue tipped with the fire of his hatred for the whites.

Chief Joseph was worried as he sensed the angry feeling among the Indians. Rebellion could break out easily today, he told himself. And rebellion meant bullets from the soldiers. He must do what he could to keep peace to save the lives of his people. He rose to speak in council.

"I am ready to talk today," he said with his usual grave dignity. "I have been in a great many councils, but I am no wiser. The Indians are as they were made by the Great Spirit, and the white men cannot change us. I do not believe that the Great Spirit Chief gave one kind of man the right to tell another kind of man what he must do."

Toohulhulzote jumped to his feet impatiently. "The Great Spirit Chief made the world as it is," he shouted, his tones a rasping insult to General Howard. "I do not see where you get your authority to say that we shall not live where he has placed us."

"The United States has set aside this large reservation for you and your children that you may live and prosper in peace," General Howard said firmly. "Do you intend to come upon the reservation peaceably? Or shall I put you there with my soldiers?"

"What person pretends," the old man raged, "to divide the land and put me on it?"

"I am the man," Howard answered, instantly stern. "I stand here for the President. My orders are plain and will be executed."

Chief Joseph listened in distress to the bad words that went on between the two, but he could not interfere. The Nez Perces had chosen Toohulhulzote as their speaker.

Finally General Howard, angered by the old Indian's

64

insolence, ordered Toohulhulzote put in the guard-house. The young warriors leaped to their feet. Bewildered whispers turned into enraged words.

"The white chief insults us," they said. "He arrests our speaker!"

Chief Joseph was on his feet also. He knew that not only General Howard's life, but the lives of his men, rested on the thin edge of decision. If trouble should start, the Nez Perces could easily kill General Howard. But the soldiers standing all about armed with guns would turn those guns on the Indians. Joseph had ordered the warriors to come to the council unarmed. All his people would be killed. He whirled to face his young men.

"Wait," he commanded, his voice ringing out above the confusion. "Do not fight. This is not the time. Do not kill."

The warriors muttered, but they subsided. Toohulhulzote, violent in his rage, was led into the guard-house. Chief Joseph turned then to speak to the white men.

"I am going to talk now," he said with firm dignity. "I do not care whether you arrest me or not." He turned his back on the general and spoke soothing words to his people. "The arrest of Toohulhulzote was wrong, but we will not resent the insult. We were invited to

65

this council to express our hearts, and we have done so. We can do no more."

Joseph knew that the Nez Perces had lost their cause. The bearded general was too strong. He had revealed his power. And behind him stood the strength of the United States Army. What could the Indians do against so many soldiers? The Nez Perces would lose the lands that the Great Spirit Chief had given them. They must come upon the reservation.

"We must yield," he counseled his people. "The soldiers are too many. If we fight, we die."

White Bird and Looking Glass also wanted peace above war, but their hearts were angry.

That night Chief Joseph felt the air heavy with the sorrow of his defeated people. He could not sleep for thinking of the hills and valleys of his loved home. At dawn rain fell.

"The skies weep with us," Joseph said to himself.

At ten the next morning the skies cleared. Joseph, White Bird and Looking Glass rode with General Howard over the reservation to choose lands for their people.

Up the Lapwai Valley they rode toward the mouth of Sweetwater Creek. High brown hills, rounded and barren, folded down toward the valley. Sadly Joseph thought of the blue waters of Wallowa Lake and the

66

cool pine-clad mountains. Here in this dry country his people would not be happy.

"When you come upon the reservation," General Howard said, pointing out some good land to Joseph, "I will move off these white settlers and give you their farms."

Joseph shook his head. "No. I have never taken what did not belong to me. I will not now."

Finally he chose land near the plain of Kamiah on the Clearwater River. He wanted to be close to White Bird, who had picked land there. Looking Glass chose grazing lands for his people in the same area.

"You have thirty days to move to the reservation," General Howard told Chief Joseph.

Thirty days, he thought. Thirty suns for his men to collect thousands of horses from ten thousand hills! Thirty days to move the women and the children and the life possessions of the band across eighty miles of rough trail to the reservation! And there was the Snake to cross, the devil river swollen with spring rain and melting snow from the mountains.

"Why are you in such a hurry?" he protested. "I cannot get ready to move in thirty days. Our stock is scattered over a hundred miles of land. The Snake River is very high. Let us wait until fall. The river will be low then."

"If you let the time run over by one day," Howard

threatened, "soldiers will come to drive you on the reservation. And cattle outside the reservation at that time will fall into the hands of the white settlers."

Heavy of heart, Chief Joseph rode across the hills to the Valley of the Winding Waters—his home that was to be his home no more.

7. WAR WILL COME

In WALLOWA CHIEF JOSEPH called a council meeting of all the Lower Nez Perces. He was their head chief, but he could not force a move so tragic for his people without the consent of the band as a whole.

"Let us fight," the young men said angrily. "Let us not be driven from our homes like tame cattle! We will give General Howard the war he wants."

Chief Joseph set himself against the war talk with all his words of wisdom and all the power of his leadership.

"We have not sixty warriors," he said. "And the United States has thousands of trained soldiers to fight us. We have not even enough guns so that each warrior can fight with one. Will you make war against the white soldiers with bows and arrows?"

He was taunted with cowardice, and he bowed his head.

"You promised your father to protect his grave with your life," a young warrior scoffed. "Will you leave that grave unguarded now?"

A broken promise was considered a broken law by the Nez Perces. Chief Joseph suffered even this slur upon his honor.

"Better to leave my father's grave undefended," he said, "than to stain the ground above it with the blood of his people."

There was more angry war talk, but Chief Joseph kept on with his plea for peace. He had been fighting many years for his people, not with guns but with words. Words must serve him now. He must persuade his people to live in peace even if he risked his chieftainship. He knew that he could be deposed. If most of his people refused his decision, they could by tribal law choose another chief. But talk for peace he must.

"If war would do any good," he told them reasonably, "then I would want war. But war will bring only death. We cannot win. If we fight, we will lose Wallowa anyway. We will lose our lives as well—and the lives of our women and children."

When the council finally listened to his logic and voted to move to the reservation peaceably, no man there was sadder than Chief Joseph. He had won his battle of words. He had saved the lives of his people. But the thought of leaving the Valley of the Winding Waters made a cold sickness grow around his heart.

However, he put his grief aside and gave the orders to begin the roundup of half-wild cattle and horses that had grazed over ten thousand hills and gullies of Wallowa since the fall before. He sent out a hundred riders to search the sage-covered hills, the hidden mountain meadows, the brush-filled creek bottoms.

"A six months' task," he told Ollocot, "and we must crowd it into only thirty suns of time."

"A-aa," Ollocot agreed mournfully. "We will leave many good horses and cattle behind. We will lose more crossing the Snake."

"And on the reservation there will not be grass enough to feed even what stock we can save. Our people will be poor in a few years."

The men herded what cattle and horses they could find to the mouth of the Imnaha, where that river poured into the Snake. Here the women were waiting, household goods piled high on the river bank.

Bitter grief was in Chief Joseph's heart as he turned away from the Valley of the Winding Waters and faced the task ahead. Here was the Snake to be crossed. The Snake was no tame river at any time; now it was a muddy torrent, fed by melting snows from the mountains. As he looked at it, the river seemed to foam and

71

snarl and roar in rage. But he gave orders in a firm voice to begin the crossing.

He watched while buffalo hides, hairy side up, were spread on the ground. Green willow poles, as thick as a thumb, were laid across the hides. Then poles and hides were bent together and lashed to other poles which had been formed into a large circle. On these rafts the women piled teepee mats, cooking pots, buffalo robes, food, and clothing.

"Take one raft across," Chief Joseph said to four young men who were stout swimmers.

They led their horses to the water's edge. Mounting and taking a firm grip on the corners of the raft, the braves forced their horses into the icy current.

In stony silence, Chief Joseph watched as the yellow river, thick with mud, clutched at the swimmers. Horses and rafts were swept downstream for yards. Great logs boiled up out of the water for a strike at the riders. Trees, uprooted by the flood, reached out to sweep them from their saddles. The horses found footing at last and struggled, dripping and spent, out of the river on the Idaho side.

After this trial trip little children were roped to the tops of the loads. Chief Joseph tightened the ropes that bound his twelve-year-old daughter, Sound-of-Running-Feet, to a raft.

72

War Will Come

"Hang tight to the ropes," he told her. "If you are swept away, I will ride in after you."

He turned then to his wife when it was her turn to cross with the other women who rode the flood with their babies secure in cradleboards. He was concerned for she was soon to bear another child. He said no word of fear when she smiled at him. She must take her chances with the other women. But he sighed with relief when he saw her raft land safely.

Raft after frail raft made the fearful crossing. By the end of the day all the Nez Perces were on the Idaho shore. Not one life had been fed the hungry river, Joseph thought.

But the next day he saw the poverty of his band begin. The horses were rounded up and stampeded straight into the river in a frenzied rush of thundering hoofs. Once in the current all swam stoutly enough for the opposite shore. But many old horses were swept down the river. Many wobbly little colts were sucked under by the current or dashed against the murderous rocks. Only the strongest horses landed on the other side.

The cattle had an even harder time. The old and sick, the fresh cows, most of the calves, were swept away or sucked under in the whirlpools.

Chief Joseph frowned when the final count was

73

made. Of the thousands of horses and cattle, less than fifteen hundred had survived.

"There will be grass enough on the reservation to feed our herds now," he said grimly. "Drive the stock up the trail to high ground. We will herd them here on the south side of the Salmon. Leave men to guard the herd. We will move on to Tolo Lake."

All of the Nez Perces of the Non-treaty bands had planned to meet before marching together to the reservation. The meeting place was at the head of a deep, rocky gorge that the Indians called Split Rocks.

As he neared the place, Chief Joseph saw that White Bird and his people already were encamped. Toohulhulzote was there, still smarting under his arrest. Chief Looking Glass and some of his people had left their gardens on the Clearwater to come and welcome the other Non-treaty bands to the reservation. Gravely Chief Joseph greeted his brother chiefs. Not even this meeting with friends could give him joy now that the Valley of Winding Waters had been left behind.

With little interest he watched the young men racing their horses and gambling away the time. He saw the women work at gathering camas, whose roots they would steam and grind for bread. The hours were running too swiftly toward a future he did not want, Joseph felt. And he put off giving the order to enter the reservation. Until the last hour of the appointed time he would let his people enjoy their freedom.

However, his concern grew as he listened to the men in council talk of their wrongs, of their losses, of their grief at leaving the mountains and green valleys of Wallowa, the canyons and hills of the Salmon River country. The talk began to get out of hand, and Joseph's concern turned to alarm. White Bird's men, eager for war, talked of battle. Old Toohulhulzote made long speeches telling of his wrongs.

Fearful that all this hotheaded talk might lead to war, Chief Joseph rose to his feet. Again he spoke for peace, urging the aroused men to remember the women and children.

"All will be killed," he said. "The soldiers are too strong for us. Fighting will not win back our lands."

Again he persuaded the council to vote for peace. But he knew that he talked, not from his own sorely angered heart, but from his mind—a mind that recognized the folly of war.

His fears lulled by the council vote, he turned to the care of his family. Exhausted by the crossing of the Snake, Toma Alwawinmy lay ill in the women's lodge awaiting the arrival of her baby.

"Perhaps some fresh beef will give her strength," Joseph told Ollocot. "Let us cross the Salmon again

75

and ride back to the beef herd. We will butcher and bring some beef."

Ollocot agreed. They set out, taking with them four men, Ollocot's wife Fair Land, and Joseph's daughter. They stayed for several days, for Joseph found that he was glad to get away from the big camp with its talk of war. When they rode back, twelve pack horses were laden with fresh beef.

As they neared the camp, Joseph saw a man riding fast to meet them.

"It is Two Moons," Ollocot said.

"He would not ride so fast unless he brings news of trouble," Joseph said, alarmed. "Two Moons is a brave man. He does not lose his head easily."

Two Moons spurred his horse toward his chief. "War has come," he shouted. "Three white men killed. White blood spilled."

Chief Joseph could not believe it. He had left camp only when he was certain that the war talk was over.

"Tell me," he said.

"It was Wahlitits. He started a war. After you left, the young men made a war parade. Wahlitits rode his horse over a woman's camas root drying in the sun. Yellow Grizzly Bear spoke angry words to him. 'Look where you ride,' he said. 'You play brave and ride over my woman's food. If you are so brave, why is your

76

father's death unavenged?' Yellow Grizzly Bear shamed
Wahlitits before all the people."

Chief Joseph could guess the rest of the story.
Wahlitits—Shore Ice—belonged to the Salmon River
band, but all the Nez Perces knew his story. He had
long brooded over the killing of his father by a white
man. The white man had asked Chief Eagle Robe for
land in the Salmon Canyon. The chief had given the
land generously. The white man had taken more land.
Eagle Robe had objected and had tried to stop the
white man from plowing. The white man had shot the
Indian. Before he died, Eagle Robe had made his son
promise not to seek revenge.

"Let the white man live his life," Eagle Robe had
said.

Shore Ice had kept his promise. But the unavenged
death of his father was a slur upon Indian honor, and
the youth had brooded over his disgrace. Chief Joseph
knew that Yellow Grizzly Bear's taunt had been the
spark that set off the young man's anger, already
aroused against the white men by the war talk.

"What has Shore Ice done?" Joseph asked fearfully.

"He slipped away from camp. He took his cousins
Red Moccasin Tops and Swan Necklace with him.
They killed four white men, all enemies to the Indians.
They stole horses. Swan Necklace came back this
morning to tell what they had done."

Thunder Rolling

"The murderers are not of our band," Joseph said hopefully. "They are White Bird's braves. My people cannot be blamed. There need not be war."

Two Moons shook his head. "It is too late for peace. The people are for war now. Wahlitits' uncle Big Dawn jumped on his horse and rode around the camp. He boasted, 'Now you will have to fight. No more time for talk. War is begun! Prepare for war! Prepare for war!' Most of the people are for war now."

Without another word Chief Joseph and Ollocot rode fast back to camp, leaving the others to bring the pack horses. Joseph called another council at once to plead for peace. White Bird's three young men had disobeyed the will of the council, but the old chief was half ready to back up the actions of his hotbloods. The council refused to vote for peace.

Joseph still hoped to persuade the council, but that night seventeen war-hungry braves joined Shore Ice and Red Moccasin Tops in a second raid. More white men were killed. Women were injured and children wounded. The beautiful Salmon Canyon became a trap for its white settlers, a grave for some of them.

When news of this second raid was carried back to the camp, Joseph knew that peace talk was of no more use. War had come.

Chief Looking Glass, whose lands were on the reservation, decided that he wanted none of this fighting

78

for his own people. Hastily he moved his band back to the Clearwater. White Bird's band moved to Cottonwood Creek. There they thought they could defend themselves if soldiers came.

"Our people want to go to Cottonwood, too," Ollocot told Chief Joseph. "What can we do?"

"Let us ride among them and talk peace," Joseph replied, for he could not give up. "We will do what we can."

He rode among his frightened people. "Do not go," he called out so that all could hear. "Let us stay here. We are not to blame. If soldiers come, we will talk peace to them."

But this time Chief Joseph could not sway his people to his will. He did not blame them. They were homeless and desperate. They went on packing their teepees and household goods, and they would not listen.

Soon there were only three lodges left in Split Rocks —Joseph's, Ollocot's, and the women's teepee where Toma Alwawinmy lay with her new baby. Sadly Chief Joseph gave the order for the move to follow his people. War could not be prevented. The time for peace had gone by.

"We must go to Lapwai," urged Young Whistasket, brother to Toma Alwawinmy. "We will be safe on the reservation. You were not here when the white men were killed. You need not go with the rest."

Thunder Rolling

"I can hardly do that," Joseph answered sorrowfully. "My place is with my people now. They have many grievances, but war will bring them more. I must stay with them."

He knew only too well that war would come quickly now. The thoughtless deed of three inflamed youths, and those not even of his own band, had started his people toward their destruction. He was their chief. If it was war they chose, then he must help fight. All his life had been a battle for peace. Now he must resolutely put his foot on the trail that led to war.

The gathering storm, with its cold wind of danger that he had sensed for so long, had broken at last, he thought. His *wyakin* had given him the name Thunder-Rolling-in-the-Mountains. Now he must live up to that name. And Toma Alwawinmy would learn the meaning of her name—Driven-Before-a-Cold-Storm. Even his young daughter Sound-of-Running-Feet must now be true to her name.

8. THE WHITE BIRD BATTLE

Before Chief Joseph was ready to leave Split Rocks, he learned that the frightened Nez Perces had not stayed in the Cottonwood Canyon. Excited and alarmed by the threat of war, many had not even unpacked their teepee mats or household goods. They had crossed the hills to a safer place deep in the canyon of the Salmon River at the mouth of White Bird Creek.

Chief Joseph moved at once to the canyon. He was the head chief of his own band, but he must now plan with White Bird, for their people had joined forces.

Joseph regretted that he was not a war chief. Nez Perce war chiefs were chosen by the band for unusual bravery and daring in actual battle conflict with enemy bands. Since he had been old enough to fight, there had been no wars. And only once as an adult had he

81

gone to the buffalo country. On that trip his people had met no enemy bands. All of his training had been aimed toward the making of a diplomat who could deal in council with the white men.

He knew that now the chosen war chiefs would take over the leadership of the warriors in the battle so sure to come. He would not have command in those battles, but he would have words to say in council. He determined that he would talk always for peace, or at least for as little bloodshed as possible. And he would still be the leader of his people in every matter except actual battle.

When he arrived at the canyon, he learned that the war chiefs had sent out scouts to watch the roads between Lewiston and two small settlements, Grangeville and Mount Idaho, on the edge of Camas Prairie not far from the Salmon Canyon. He remembered all the roads and trails across the prairie. White men would be riding fast across the spring mud to take the news of the uprising to General Howard and his troopers at Lewiston.

Orders for the Indian scouts had been only that they must stop all messengers between the towns. But Chief Joseph soon learned that the scouts had attacked freighters who were taking a wagonload of whiskey to Mount Idaho. The freighters had been killed, and the Indians had drunk the whiskey. Inflamed, they had

82

found settlers to attack. More white men had been injured or killed. Chief Joseph was bitterly grieved over this senseless taking of life.

"I would have given my life," he said afterwards, "if I could have undone the killing of white men by my people."

On the night of the sixteenth of June, Chief Joseph rested with his brother Ollocot on blankets spread in the shadow of a great rock near the camp on White Bird Creek. The brothers knew from scouts that General Howard had not taken time to find out that the Indian uprising was in reality no war, but only murder by a few for personal revenge. He had ordered Captain Perry to move at once from Lewiston with a hundred soldiers to attack the Indian camp in the canyon.

Indian scouts hidden behind ridges and knolls had watched the soldiers in their forced march across Camas Prairie. Signal fires flaming on the hills now told Chief Joseph of the approach of the soldiers. He knew, as he rested and waited for the dawn, that Captain Perry and his troopers had left Grangeville to cross the mountain trail to the Canyon of the Salmon.

Joseph smiled as he thought of that mountain the white men must cross. Three thousand feet below the summit lay the dark floor of the canyon. Captain Perry no doubt thought it was going to be a simple matter to surprise the Indian camp at dawn. But he did not know of the many rocky ridges and gullies, of the steep slopes down which his men must ride.

The black night lay all about the two brothers. The canyon walls were dark shadows closing them in. Joseph lay wide awake, savoring those last few hours of peace. He thought of his wife, lying in a lodge apart, attended by the women. The new child was a girl. He had hoped it would be a boy. Suffering would be the lot of both his daughters—and of all the women of his tribe from now on. This new life had begun in a troubled world. Many suns of hardship must shine upon this new girl-child's head.

Suddenly the cry of a coyote split the silence of the walls above. It ended on a shrill, unnatural note. Nez Perce guards, watching from a high rock, had heard the sound of the iron-clad hoofs of a hundred horses. Joseph and Ollocot leaped to their feet and tried to see through the darkness that hid even the high hills.

A horse scrambled down the rough trail. It was Seeskoomke, old No-Feet, calling out as he rode, "Soldiers coming! Soldiers coming this way!"

Chief Joseph watched intently as the first gray line of summer dawn placed ghostly fingers upon the rim of the canyon whose floor still lay in darkness. As the light grew, he saw the tiny figures of soldiers. Their horses were picking a dangerous way down the rocky gullies that led to the valley.

The White Bird Battle

"Many soldiers," Joseph said quietly.

He knew what Captain Perry could not know: that although the floor of the canyon looked close, two hours of hard riding lay ahead of the troopers.

"We have plenty of time to prepare for war," he told Ollocot. "Go tell White Bird and the other chiefs. Rouse the camp."

White Bird, Toohulhulzote and the other war chiefs returned with Ollocot. The chiefs held council.

"Let us cross over the Salmon," one chief urged. "The water is high. The white men cannot cross it. We can fight from cover."

"No," said another war chief. "If we must fight, let us fight them here. Time enough to cross the Salmon if we are whipped here."

Chief Joseph said nothing, for he did not want this war to start. All finally agreed to fight the soldiers in the canyon. Chief Joseph rode fast toward his own band to give the orders to prepare for battle. He watched the camp come to quick life. Horses were brought in close. Trained war ponies were caught and held in readiness by the young boys. The women were given orders to hold the best of the remaining herd ready should the fighters need remounts. Warriors stripped to their breech clouts for battle. Armed for war, each stood at his horse's head, waiting for orders.

Thunder Rolling

The war chiefs told their men the plan that had been made.

"A-aa," the warriors murmured. "The plan is good."

The sun rose higher. The soldiers were coming down a defile among the rounded hills and rocky gullies. The silence was broken by the sudden *Caw! Caw!* of a crow. Scouts hidden in the rocks were telling the chiefs, "Soldiers are coming close!"

"It is time," Chief Joseph said.

Ollocot, wearing the broad sash of a commander, loped his fine cream-colored horse toward a high butte, shaped like a loaf of bread. The butte rose to the right of the approaching soldiers. Behind him rode thirty warriors. All were soon hidden behind the butte.

Chief Joseph watched Two Moons with twelve warriors gallop to the foot of a long draw that led up to the left of the soldiers.

Moxmox and a few of the most skilled riders held the remaining war horses well to the rear. The chiefs had a special plan for this group, a plan that would take daring and courage.

Among them were the Three Red Coats, fierce young braves who always had been close friends. They were Shore Ice, who had led the Salmon River murder raid, Red Moccasin Tops, and Strong Eagle. The three friends wore blanket coats of red, cut alike.

86

The White Bird Battle

"We shall be brothers in battle," they had boasted. "We will fight as one warrior."

Joseph had smiled grimly when their chief, White Bird, had told Shore Ice with sarcasm, "You wanted this war. Now fight." Shore Ice, Joseph thought bitterly, not only had wanted this war; he had started the war.

With White Bird and the rest of the warriors, Chief Joseph took the place assigned to him, concealed behind rocks and bushes directly in the path of the advancing soldiers.

In silence he waited. He studied the battlefield before him. Directly to the front a flat bench of land rose. It was like an army saddle, he thought, with a high rocky ridge for the saddle's pommel and three rounded knolls for the cantle. On this saddle of land, he knew, the action would begin.

The crack of a rifle shot to the north jarred the stillness. A white man rode a white horse swiftly into the saddle of ground. Not a soldier, because the man wore the big white hat of the cattle rancher, Joseph decided.

"Wait," he said. "It is Chapman. He is a friend to us, married to a Nez Perce woman. There is yet a chance for peace. We will send out a peace offer."

White Bird, who was not eager to fight twice the number of the Indian warriors, agreed. Chief Joseph quickly ordered six braves to carry a white flag of truce toward Chapman.

87

"Do not shoot unless the white men fire first at you," Joseph ordered.

The braves advanced warily. Joseph scarcely drew breath for hoping. If only this war could be stopped! But Ad Chapman, who always had pretended friendship toward the Nez Perces, lifted his gun to his shoulder and fired at the advancing peace party. He missed aim.

The eleven men with him, also ranchers and businessmen from their dress, had the decency not to shoot. The braves in the peace party also held their fire, but they turned and ran back to shelter.

"They do not respect our peace offer," Chief Joseph said sadly. "There is nothing left but to fight."

There was a moment of dead silence in the canyon. The scene seemed incredibly peaceful to Joseph. An eagle wheeled above in great swooping circles. The rising sun warmed the western hills to gold. Blue mountain lupine and yellow daisies swayed in the morning breeze. But on that field in front of him the blood of his people soon would stain the ground. The Indians were outnumbered two to one, for they had less than sixty able-bodied warriors. What was worse, many of them carried only old muzzle-loading guns or bows and arrows and war clubs to fight with. But all looked in readiness.

The White Bird Battle

The purple shadows lay deep over the gully that hid Two Moons and his warriors.

Ollocot and his men made no sound behind the loaf-like butte.

The Three Red Coats, far to the rear, stood ready at their horses' heads, warriors and mounts eager for the battle signal.

Chief Joseph knew that his own warrior group was impatient for the battle to begin.

Ad Chapman fired again, aiming at the bushes behind which the peace party had disappeared. And this time the men with him also fired.

Then, out of the sky, over the hills, Chief Joseph saw many blue-coated soldiers ride into the flat of land directly in front of him. The war chief in Joseph's group raised his hand to give the signal for his men to begin the attack.

A rifle shot cracked the stillness. The bugler, riding at the head of the soldier column, reeled and fell from his saddle. Joseph began firing rapidly now with the warriors. Soon every rock and bush and hollow in front of the troopers was spitting death.

Chapman and his citizen volunteers turned and galloped to cover behind the first of the knolls that formed the cantle of the saddle battleground. But the soldiers moved into line at a trot.

89

Thunder Rolling

"We have few guns," Chief Joseph told his men. "Make every bullet count."

His men obeyed. They were good marksmen. The line of soldiers wavered. Their horses, green to battle, soon were out of hand. Many of the soldiers, confused by the deadly fire they had not expected, dismounted or were thrown from their horses. The horses galloped to the rear in panic. Joseph and his men moved slowly forward, each man fighting as he could.

Two Moons now led his warriors in a sweeping gallop up the hidden gully to surprise Chapman and his eleven men behind their knoll. These men, unused to war, fled their position in disorder, never stopping until their horses had scrambled to the rim of the canyon.

"It is good," Joseph said to old White Bird. "Now we have the soldiers flanked."

Bullets and arrows plowed into the soldiers from their own left flank. Their battle line crumbled and broke.

Instantly the Three Red Coats and the warriors who had been holding their horses in check at the Indian rear drove straight through the center of the soldiers' shattered line in a spearhead of dust and pounding hoofs. With fierce pride Chief Joseph watched these young braves, each riding low on the side of his horse with only a hand showing on the mane. They reached the rear of the soldier line. There the Three Red Coats raised a shrill, triumphant shout and began fighting with reckless frenzy.

"Watch where you aim," Joseph shouted to his men. "Do not kill our own men!"

Ollocot and his men now joined the battle from the butte to the soldiers' right.

"It is done," Joseph told White Bird. "We have the soldiers circled now."

Elated, Chief Joseph watched soldier deserters riding frantically up the gully toward the canyon's rim. He heard Captain Perry and his officers rallying the fleeing men and urging them into an orderly retreat.

"They are running," Joseph said. "We have them whipped."

On the battlefield he ordered a count made of the Nez Perces. He knew relief and joy when he learned that of the fifty or so warriors who had fought none had been killed and only three wounded.

From the bodies of thirty-three dead soldiers, the Indians took all arms and equipment that could be made useful. They took the spoils of war, but they did not scalp or mutilate the dead.

"Let the dead lie in peace," Chief Joseph said, for this was Nez Perce law.

The morning sun still shone on the floor of the canyon when he rode back to the joy-wild camp on the

White Bird. The fighting had taken a scant three hours.

The chiefs held a council just below the village of teepees. The guns taken in battle were counted. The fight had given them sixty-three guns.

"Nez Perces will not go armed with bows and arrows into another battle," Chief Joseph said. He added, "If we must fight again."

Long into the night the tom-toms beat as the warriors danced to the clash of drums and the high, shrill victory chant.

But Chief Joseph sat apart, deep in a gloom of the mind. He knew that after this battle he would have to lead his people far away. Now that white soldiers had been killed, there would no longer be either peace or freedom for his people in the country near.

9. BATTLE OF THE CLEARWATER

Two days more the Nez Perces camped in the Salmon Canyon. The peace-loving Joseph must have wished to spend more time in that lovely canyon with its grassy floors and protecting walls. But Nez Perce rifles had taken the lives of white soldiers. He knew that soldiers would soon come again in greater numbers.

The chiefs gave orders; the bands obeyed. They crossed the deep swift waters of the Salmon, clinging again to the loaded buffalo-skin rafts. Chief Joseph listened to his people as they sang the Song of Departure, for the Nez Perces sang whenever they set out upon a journey. As he listened, he thought sorrowfully

93

that his people from now on would sing many Songs of Departure. But at least in the high hills bordering the Salmon, the women and children of his tribe could sleep at night undisturbed by the alarm, "Soldiers coming!"

Scouts brought Joseph word that General Howard was massing troops at Lewiston. All the U.S. Army commands of the West, the scouts said, were sending men. The one-armed general was wise, Joseph thought. For the victory of the Nez Perces might encourage all the Indian tribes from the Cascades to the Rockies to join in the war.

Joseph and his associate chiefs knew that orders from Washington would be carried out by this stern Howard. He was an upright and honest man, a severe and forceful officer, a man of his word. Their only hope was to evade the troops and hide in the hills. On this plan Joseph, White Bird, and the war chiefs decided to act.

"The Salmon is running high," Chief Joseph said. "General Howard cannot cross it."

"But if the soldiers do cross the Salmon, then what will we do?" asked one of the chiefs.

"We will cross over again," War Chief Rainbow said. "We will keep the river between us."

"If we cross again," Joseph suggested, "we can then move east and north to the Clearwater."

Battle of the Clearwater

"A-aa, it is good," White Bird agreed. "On the Clearwater we will be on the west end of the Lolo Trail. If soldiers come, we can cross the Bitter Roots to the buffalo country. There we will be safe."

Secure across the Salmon, the Nez Perces waited for General Howard to catch up with them. A week later scouts brought word that Howard and his troops had arrived and were trying to cross the river.

"Let the soldiers cross the river if they can," Chief Joseph said. "We are not after them. They are after us. If they come to our side, they will not find us."

After two or three efforts that failed because the river was still high, Howard and his army of four hundred and fifty soldiers and one hundred scouts and packers finally succeeded in fording the Salmon.

But on the other side they found no sign of any Indian. Chief Joseph played at hide-and-seek, and the good general wore the blindfold.

Chief Joseph smiled to himself as his people recrossed the Salmon and headed for the Clearwater, taking a roundabout way. He smiled to see a fine June rain falling, and he thought of how the white army must be slipping and sliding up and down these rough hills. Their heavy guns and wagons would mire in the mud.

"General Howard will have to cross a swollen river again," Joseph said sardonically to Ollocot. "Perhaps

95

then he will remember those stern orders he gave to
our people to cross the flood of the Snake in May."

Joseph smiled again when scouts told him that the
General had kept his troops struggling to follow for
twenty miles down the Salmon until the Nez Perce's
deceiving trail had led them back to the river again.
He had tried to cross where the Indians had crossed the
second time, but he had given up and marched his men
back to the White Bird crossing. General Howard
would not be in a good humor, Joseph thought.

The chiefs stopped to hold council. There was time
for talking now. They were again at Split Rocks on the
edge of the plateau of prairie land near the settlement
of Cottonwood. Between them and the Clearwater
country to the east was a reserve troop of soldiers at
Norton's Ranch in Cottonwood.

"Let us get by them without more killing," Joseph
begged.

The council was interrupted by the sound of drum-
ming hoofs. Horses bearing Nez Perce men came galloping fast into camp.

"It is Chief Looking Glass," Joseph said. "Maybe
he has thought twice and now wants to join us."

Looking Glass flung himself from his horse and
strode into the council circle. He was hot with anger.

"Look you, my chiefs," he shouted, his arms spread,
his head back, his face grim with fury. "Two days ago

96

my camp was attacked by soldiers. I told them I had been strong for peace, but they would not listen. My horses were driven off. My lodges were burned. Our gardens on the Clearwater were trampled into the ground. Two of my people were killed. Now, my brothers, as long as I live, I will never make peace. Let us attack the soldiers at Cottonwood. Many a man dies for his dear native land, and we might as well die in battle as in any other way."

"Your people?" Joseph asked. "Where are they now?"

"Hidden deep in the mountains. We must join them. I have forty fighting men and twenty guns."

This thoughtless move on the part of General Howard, who had sent soldiers to make the attack on Looking Glass, had given the Nez Perces welcome reinforcements. Howard again had listened to false reports. He had heard that many of the Kamiah warriors were riding to join Chief Joseph. The truth was that Looking Glass and his people had wanted nothing but peace.

The next day Joseph and the other chiefs gave the orders to begin the march to the Clearwater. On the way a band of warriors swooped down on the soldiers at Norton's Ranch and killed ten.

On the following day the Nez Perces attacked a barricade hastily thrown up at Cottonwood. But this

97

time it was for the purpose of distracting the attention of the troopers. While the younger warriors attacked, Chief Joseph in full sight of the troopers hurried the women and children, the old men, the stock and the pack animals in a great sweeping circle across the prairie toward the mountains of the Clearwater. Here Looking Glass had hidden his people.

The warring Nez Perce bands joined. They made camp on the south fork of the Clearwater in a deep ravine near what is now Harpster, Idaho.

When Chief Joseph looked over the campground, he saw that it was good. Nearby were many grass-covered hills and small prairies for the grazing herds. To the east the mountains offered good hunting of elk, bear and deer. The entrance to the Lolo Trail was not far to the north. Food, good grazing, and a handy escape if they were pressed, he thought.

He knew that General Howard had come up out of the canyon and was riding to hunt down the Nez Perces. But the soldiers were days behind. Joseph thought his people were safe enough. There was time for a rest.

One day as he sat in council with the other chiefs, he heard a great echo-rousing roar. There came a strange swishing sound in the air. Something hit the ground just beyond the teepees. Soil and rocks were flung high with a clash of gravel and shattered stone.

Battle of the Clearwater

Women ran in panic from the teepees. Little children screamed.

Chief Joseph leaped to his feet. He looked up to the high hills across the river. Soldiers must be coming. And they had the big guns with them. Howard had caught up.

A scout came riding his horse fast down the slope. He waved his blanket as he forced his horse through the stream.

"Soldiers!" he shouted. "Soldiers surrounding us!"

Warriors stripped for battle and seized their guns. War chiefs shouted commands, their voices rising loud above the noise and confusion.

"Split up!" the orders rang out. "Split up. Some stay here to protect the women and children. Warriors to the left of the soldiers. Warriors to the right."

Chief Joseph seized his gun, mounted the horse that his wife brought him, and plunged to battle. Ahead of him he saw twenty young warriors led by Toolhulhulzote gallop their horses across the river sending the spray high. Up the steep hill the horses scrambled into a ravine that led to the right of the advancing bluecoats. Hastily the warriors tied their mounts in a clump of trees and hurried to the edge of the plateau to fling themselves down behind rock or bush.

It was good, Joseph thought, as he rode. Twenty warriors could hold General Howard's army until there was time to organize the battle. The Indians had been surprised. This time they had no good plan. Every man would have to fight as he could. But more warriors would come soon.

In Nez Perce warfare no man was forced to fight unless he chose. Many had remained in camp. That was good too, Joseph thought. The women and children would be protected.

"Wait," Toohulhulzote shouted.

He crawled out on the plateau. In a minute he was back.

"Many soldiers coming," he reported.

"Hurry. Build rifle pits," Joseph ordered. "There is time. Bring rocks. Pile here. We will make a fort."

Soon they had a small stone shelter. From behind it they fired at the soldiers, who had now come out on the plateau. For a time the white men were driven back.

Over the edge of the pit Chief Joseph saw another party of warriors galloping their horses up a ravine that led to the left of Howard's men. Here also rock shelters were hastily built.

The soldiers, advancing now, were caught between Indian crossfire. They dropped on their faces and crawled bravely forward, the long grass their only shelter.

When the first desperate skirmishing had simmered

100

down, Chief Joseph could see that the soldiers had formed their line in a long two-mile semicircle. Its center was thrust forward toward the river bluff. His own men were entrenched in an encircling half-moon about the soldiers' line.

The tips of the half-moon were the two ravines, one to the left, one to the right. From these, Indian sharp-shooters, hidden behind boulders and the rifle pits, were sending bullets into the soldier line. Ahead of the troopers more Nez Perces were fighting from the fringe of rocks and trees that marked the river bank. Soldier line and Indian line made two great half-moons, the arcs fitting into each other.

"It is good," Joseph said to Ollocot, who was fighting beside him. "We had not time to plan, but it is good."

All day long Chief Joseph fought. He rode back and forth along the line. He was everywhere, directing and helping where he could. Never did he leave the lines for one moment. Two of his mounts were killed, but he snatched a third from another warrior and rode the line again. Wherever his men wavered, he was there to urge them on with his fierce cries. The soldiers thought he was the big war chief of the day and held their aim on him. But his *wyakin* was strong that day to guard him. He received not so much as a scratch.

In the lulls of the fighting he had time to notice that his people were standing up to the test of the big guns.

Thunder Rolling

Nez Perce warriors never had faced the raking fire of the Gatling guns nor the booming of the howitzers. He hoped that they would remember the instruction of their fathers: "It is good to die in battle. It is good to die for your rights, for your own land."

They were remembering. Each warrior was sending his bullets wisely. Many times across the battlefield Joseph heard the "Echo of a Song," the Nez Perce cry which means, "I have met the enemy and taken his life."

Slowly across the sky marched the hot July sun. It hung low over the battlefield at last, a dull red ball gleaming through a cloud of acrid gun smoke and rolling dust.

Night came down, clear and cold. The two forces faced each other in silence. No shots were fired now. The soldiers, Joseph knew, would not dare to light campfires for fear of Indian bullets. His sharpshooters could hold the field all night.

Wearily he rode back to camp. There the fires burned bright all that moonless night. Joseph and the other chiefs talked to the warriors, urging them to fiercer fighting with the dawn. Medicine men beat the tom-toms and raised the war chant. Warriors danced the war dance. A woman who had lost her husband in the day's battle raised the wail of the Death Song. Sadly Chief Joseph wondered how many times he would hear that death chant before his people could live in peace once more.

Dawn came. With the sun the fighting began again. When Chief Joseph rode to the battlefield, he saw that during the night hours the soldiers had made barricades. Now their shooting seemed to make one continual roar in his ears.

All day the battle went on. In the afternoon Joseph spied a small dust cloud rolling up over the horizon far to the soldiers' rear.

"More soldiers coming!" he shouted. "Stop them. No, it is mules with ammunition and food for the soldiers. Stop the mules."

Watching, he saw warriors ride at full speed out from the sheltering ravines. They whipped their horses toward the dust cloud. But General Howard had seen also. He sent a troop of cavalry galloping out on the plateau.

"They will get between our men and the supply train," Joseph said to Ollocot.

The battle stopped as both sides watched the pack mules bounding through the swirling dust. Joseph cried out in anger when the supply train rolled its cloud of dust safely behind the soldier line. A long cheer of relief went up from the soldiers.

And now came what Chief Joseph knew was the turning point of the battle. The troop of soldiers which had dashed out to bring in the supply train wheeled suddenly and whirled back. This cavalry made a surprise attack on the head of the right ravine across from Joseph's position.

He saw the warriors there, confused by the unexpected sortie, waver before the oncoming soldiers. Waves of blue-coated soldiers were surging down upon his people. He spurred his horse around the line.

"We are not whipped," he shouted. "Let us fight!"

The attack was repulsed, but many of the warriors wanted to quit this fighting that seemed to get nowhere.

"Our camp is not being attacked," they said. "Why should we fight up here on the plateau? Let us go to the camp."

Vaulting on their horses, the warriors dashed down the hills. There were too many soldiers, too many big guns. Joseph saw that the soldiers were rolling up the Indian line in front of them as the wave of blue advanced. He knew that the battle was lost. Riding at reckless speed, he dashed back to the camp to warn the women and children.

"Leave what is not packed," he shouted. "Make yourselves safe. Quick! Up that canyon there!"

He kept urging his people to speed until the pack horses were whipped up the canyon. Travois, loaded with what goods the women could throw on, were piled high. Children clung to the lashings and yelled, whipping the horses to speed. Food was left cooking on the fires. The good odor of roasted antelope wasted itself on the air.

Not until the camp had emptied itself in dust, noise, and confusion did Joseph ride after his people. Then he kept urging haste, calling out commands, trying to bring order out of the retreat.

He did not know that his wife had been left behind with her new baby. He had given her warning and thought she was ahead with the first women to ride away. But Toma Alwawinmy had gone back to her teepee for some prized possession.

When he heard horses riding fast behind him, he turned quickly, his gun at his shoulder. Soldiers must be catching up with the band. But it was Toma Alwawinmy riding with his young cousin Yellow Wolf.

"We were left behind," she told her husband. "I was weak and could not mount alone with my baby. Yellow Wolf came late from the battle. He helped me, or our baby would not now be safe."

Chief Joseph nodded his relief and thanks to his cousin, and the three rode on. Behind them as they rode, Joseph could hear the shells of the great guns bursting in the empty camp. The smoke of deserted cooking fires rose lazily in the clear mountain air. Empty teepees stood by the river.

105

"We had to leave buffalo mats behind," Toma Alwawinmy said, "and teepee poles and mats. And all the meat dried and jerked for our winter food."

"There will be no more warm beds for the Nez Perces," Joseph said, "nor much good food for Nez Perce hunger."

Sadly he rode to join his retreating people. And as he rode, the plaintive song of the Nez Perces on the march drifted back to him through the canyon.

10. THE FEARFUL TRAIL

CHIEF JOSEPH and his people retreated to Kamiah. As he rode, he thought with grief of defeat. But they had not been whipped, he told himself. With less than a hundred warriors they had held General Howard and his four hundred and fifty soldiers for two days on the plateau. Only four Nez Perces had been killed and six wounded; but General Howard, the scouts said, had lost thirteen men and counted twice that many wounded. When the soldiers poured down from the bluff, they had found only an empty camp with not an Indian to take captive. The women and children were safe. No, the Nez Perces had not been whipped. They had what they wanted—escape and a free trail ahead of them.

The Indians moved on to Weippe, a lush green

meadow set in the darker rim of the forest. At the eastern side there was a slash in the ranks of great pines that marched in millions up the high Bitter Root Mountains. This slash marked the opening of the Lolo Trail.

Joseph's thoughts were bitter as he rode out onto the meadow. Here his fathers had welcomed the first white men to Nez Perce land. And now here on this meadow Nez Perce chiefs must meet in council to decide whether to fight, surrender, or flee from the white men —the men who had taken Nez Perce land from its owners.

That night the council fire leaped high, its red glow touching the rim of the forest. The talk was long and bitter.

"I have sent a peace party back to General Howard," Joseph told the assembled chiefs.

"And what are his terms?" they asked.

"All men to give themselves up and be tried by the white men," Joseph answered sadly.

He knew what this would mean for himself and for all the other chiefs—the firing squad. Always the chiefs were held responsible for the actions of all their people.

There was silence around the fire. Each chief had his own thoughts. Life was pleasant. Life was sweet to Joseph also, but the safety of his people and their

108

right to live in peace on lands that they knew meant more to him than life.

"I will surrender," he offered. "Perhaps that will satisfy General Howard, and he will not ask for more lives."

"No," said the chiefs, refusing his offer. "We will stay together."

"Let us go to the buffalo country," proposed Looking Glass. "The Crows are our friends. We will be safe there."

"A-aa, let us go to the buffalo country," agreed White Bird and Toohulhulzote. "In Montana we will find a new home."

Chief Joseph felt grief clutch at his heart like an iron hand. When his band took the first step on the Lolo Trail, they would be leaving the land of their fathers. They might never be able to return. Above all else he had wanted peace for his people, but not a peace that would send them wandering homeless in lands strange to them.

"No!" he said, his voice ringing loud and clear to the rim of the forest. "What are we fighting for? Is it our lives? No. It is for this fair land where the bones of our fathers are buried. Some of you tried to say once that I was afraid of the whites. Stay here with me now and we will have plenty of fighting. We will put our women behind us in these mountains and die on our own land. I would rather do that than run I know not where."

"No," Looking Glass insisted stubbornly. "Let us go to the buffalo country."

"A-aa," voted the others. "The buffalo country."

Joseph bowed his head for a moment while his mind made a quick picture of Wallowa. He might never again see the snow-capped mountains of Wallowa shouldering the blue-bright sky of his home land.

"A-aa," he agreed then, "let us go to the buffalo country."

The council had decided. It was now his duty as chief to lead his people where they willed to go. Sadly he gave his own band the orders to pack for the long march over the fearful Lolo Trail.

At least the Lolo was not new to the Nez Perces, Joseph thought, but it was no easy trail at any time. This march was to be no carefree ride of hunters crossing the mountains to shoot buffalo. This would be the race of his people for freedom and for life. They must drive a herd of twenty-five hundred horses. Women and children and old men must ride the cruel trail. Wounded warriors no longer could be carried lashed to travois, but must take their chances and their pain on horseback. He shuddered when he thought of that steep and boulder-blocked trail.

He knew also that his burdened people would not

ride unhindered. Close on their heels would be General Howard and his army.

The chiefs, learning that the general finally had crossed the Clearwater, sent a party of young men back over the trail to raid white ranchers and to ambush a troop of soldiers riding to join the general. The ambush failed, but General Howard was delayed long enough to give the Nez Perces time to get well up the trail.

Up, up Chief Joseph climbed with his people across the Bitter Root Range. They rode through tangled forests, across great fallen trees matted together, over rocks and around huge boulders.

"Do not take time to cut through the tangles," he told them. "Push the horses through."

Many an exhausted war pony was left behind to forage for itself. Many a horse fell with a broken leg.

"The lives of our people are more important than horses," Joseph said. "We have many horses."

At the night stops he did his best to make his people comfortable. He saw that they camped by clear cold springs in mountain meadows where the horses could feed on the long grass. Since all of their cattle had been left behind on the Salmon, he sent out hunters to bring down with silent arrows the plentiful elk and deer. He ordered fires left burning all night to drive away the creeping mountain cold, for the Nez Perces had no lodges now. Most of their lodge poles and

111

teepee mats had been left behind at the Battle of the Clearwater. At night the women rolled the children in the few remaining buffalo robes and kept them near the fires for warm sleeping.

Each dawn Chief Joseph started his band on the march. Over rock slides, through swamps, in rain and fog and mist that made the narrow trail slippery and dangerous, they climbed up until the way wound along the ridgetops.

Sixteen miles a day was the most that they could make. Joseph knew that the soldiers could make more —perhaps forty miles a day. They would ride unhindered by families and possessions.

"We must hurry," he told his people. "We are not safe until we cross the pass into Montana."

On the fifth day the trail grew steeper, rougher. Jagged rocks made the horses' feet bleed. Stunted trees, whipped by wind and storm, clung to scant ground among vast boulders. They were nearing the summit, Joseph knew. But always he kept urging faster marching. As his horse picked a perilous way along the high ridges, he watched the trail below for the approach of the soldiers.

He was glad when they topped the pass at last and started down the mountains. But the ledges along which the trail wound here were more narrow and steeper. If a horse slipped, death waited below on the jumble of rocks and boulders.

"Dismount," he gave orders. "Lead your horses. Cling close to the cliff side if you wish to live."

The end of the cruel trail was only a day's ride ahead when they came one night to a wide, grassy meadow with the mountains rising high above. Scouts brought Joseph the welcome news that General Howard was now far behind. The soldiers and their mounts were not accustomed to such a trail as the Lolo, Joseph thought with grim satisfaction.

"Let us rest here," he said. "The women and children are tired. We are in need of food. There are hot springs in the meadow for bathing. There is grass for the horses. Let us rest."

But that night scouts that had been sent ahead came riding into camp.

"Soldiers in front of us!" they cried. "They are building a fort. They have us headed off. Soldiers ahead of us in the trail!"

Chief Joseph knew that the trail to the east crawled through a narrow canyon with high mountains coming down close on either side. If soldiers had blocked that deep cut, his people were stopped dead on the trail.

What he did not know was that General Howard had sent a telegram to Captain Rawn at Missoula, Montana. The captain had been ordered to head off the Nez Perces on the Montana side of the pass. With forty soldiers and a hundred citizen volunteers, Captain Rawn had moved to the canyon and built a barricade across it.

"We cannot go back," Chief Joseph told the chiefs. "General Howard is back there. We do not want another battle. We must go on and take our chances with these new soldiers. Perhaps we can persuade them to let us go by."

Joseph, White Bird, and Looking Glass arranged a parley with Captain Rawn. Looking Glass was chosen to speak because for years he had ridden through this country on his way to the buffalo hunting. In Montana he was known to the white ranchers and well liked.

"We are friends to the people of Montana," Looking Glass told the captain. "Let us pass through. We wish only to go to the buffalo country."

"You may pass through," Rawn said firmly, "if you will surrender your arms, your ammunition, and your horses."

"We do not come to fight the white men," Joseph said, joining in the parley. "We have been driven from our homes. We go to the buffalo country to find ourselves another home."

"Your guns, your ammunition, your horses—and you can go through," Rawn persisted.

"We cannot give you our guns and horses," Joseph

argued. "We must have guns to hunt with, horses to ride. But we will not use our guns against you or the settlers, if you will only let us go by."

Captain Rawn refused. The chiefs drew aside to talk.

"If we wait here," Joseph said, "General Howard will catch up with us. Soldiers will be in front of us and behind us. There will be more war. That is what the white men want."

And now, as the chiefs watched the white men, they saw that many of those not dressed in the blue coats of the soldiers were mounting their horses and riding off. The rancher citizens were quietly going home.

"They know that we will not harm them," Looking Glass said shrewdly. "They know that Nez Perces always keep a promise. They know that we have goods to trade and money, and they want our money."

"The forty soldiers are not leaving," Joseph remarked. "The way is still blocked."

"We can whip them—only forty soldiers," said the young hotbloods among the Indians. "Let us fight!"

"No," Joseph said. "We want no more war."

None of the other chiefs wanted another battle. All they wanted was to reach Montana where they could live in peace.

Chief Joseph smiled. "Let us be like Coyote the Crafty. If we cannot go through, let us go around."

The chiefs glanced up at the cliffs. "There is no way."

"We will find a way," Joseph said.

Early the next morning a few warriors were sent to climb the rocks close to the fort and to fire at the barricade. While the warriors were distracting the attention of the soldiers, Joseph started his people on their difficult ride. In single file, singing the high, weird Song of Departure, they crawled like a line of moving beetles across the face of the cliff to the left. But they were well out of gun range. Joseph smiled to himself as he thought how the helpless soldiers must be swearing in their beards.

The path, winding through a chain of cross canyons, brought the Nez Perces peacefully out into the Lolo Canyon far on the Montana side of the soldiers.

Chief Joseph turned southward to avoid the town of Missoula. Before him lay the broad reaches of the Bitter Root Valley, where his people were known and liked by the friendly ranchers.

He thought that General Howard and war and the shedding of blood had been left far behind. There would be no more fighting. Peace and a new home in the buffalo country lay ahead.

116

11. BATTLE OF THE BIG HOLE

CHIEF JOSEPH allowed his band to move slowly up the valley of the Bitter Root, trading with the friendly white people, buying supplies of flour, sugar, and tobacco. He traveled only fourteen miles or so a day, making long camps so that the tired and foot-sore horses could rest and grow fat on the rich meadow-land grass.

He had no heart for any more fighting, nor much interest in where the three bands of Nez Perces traveled.

"While we were fighting for our own country," he said in council, "there was reason to fight. But while we are here, I would not have anything to say for fighting, for this is not my country. Since we have left our country, it matters little where we go."

117

Thunder Rolling

His thoughts were on his loved Valley of the Winding Waters. Memories rode with him—bitter memories of his father, whose grave he had left unprotected. Joseph hated each added mile that grew between him and his home country. Always his fear was that he might die in this strange land. His own grave, the graves of his people, like that of his father's, would lie unhonored and undefended in these unfamiliar hills.

He believed that his people were free of pursuit at last. They were well fed. They were even more or less welcome in this valley. But there was something he could not explain, only could feel—something in the air that whispered doom. Death was near.

The Nez Perces camped the night of August seventh in the valley of the Big Hole River, a green basin set down in the high mountains that form the border between Montana and Idaho. The basin is southwest of what is now the city of Butte.

It was a good camp, Joseph thought as he looked it over. The valley was laced with streams, and there were pine thickets to supply his people with new lodge poles. They would stop for the day to cut poles, he decided.

All that next day he watched, ill at ease, while the women cut lodge poles from the dense pine forests and the young boys herded the horses on the sunny meadows. The warriors fished, hunted, played games, and

118

talked. His people were happy and safe now, he tried to tell himself. Just ahead was the buffalo country, and war had been left behind. But he was still uneasy, still sensing danger.

And Chief Joseph was right in his foreboding. General Howard, still two days' march behind, again had invoked the white man's strong medicine. He had telegraphed ahead to Fort Shaw in Montana to ask for help to hold the Nez Perces until he could catch up. Colonel Gibbon had set out from the fort with a force of one hundred and forty-six men. He had sent scouts ahead to find the position of the Indian camp.

All that day while the Indians played and worked, these scouts watched. At sunset Colonel Gibbon with his large force joined the advance party. Soldiers lay hidden in the forest at the edge of the basin, ready to attack at dawn.

When the day passed peacefully, Joseph put aside his feeling that danger was near. His mind retired into sad thoughts of the home he had left.

Looking Glass, who had been leading the three bands because he knew the country of Montana so well, had no fears.

"There have been no good times since this war began," he declared. "Now danger is over. Let there be a feast night."

That evening the new lodges were set up in the meadow south of Ruby Creek, not far from the Big Hole River. Alders and willows grew thick along the stream.

Lost in his dream of Wallowa, Chief Joseph had little heart for the merrymaking. He took no part in the singing, feasting, and dancing. He sat before his teepee, listening to the tom-toms beat far into the night as both men and women gambled at their game of stick and bone, similar to "Button, button, who's got the button?" When the feasting stopped at midnight, he was glad to rest in the comfort of his new lodge.

But he could not sleep. The uneasy sense of danger returned to keep him awake. Through the small hours of the night the banked fires smoldered. Now and then a log broke and flared into flame to light the peaceful teepees of his people. Toward dawn he saw several women come from their lodges, throw fresh logs on the fires, gossip a few minutes by the flames, and then go back to the comfort of the lodges.

In the twilight of the dawn Joseph heard a dipper bird pipe out its clear ringing note from the willows by the stream. Through the opening of his teepee he saw Natalekin come out of his lodge. The nearly blind old man stretched lazily. Then he mounted a tethered pony and cantered off to the meadow to look after his horses. Joseph watched, smiling a little, as he saw the old man peer this way and that, although the horses were almost in front of his nose.

120

Battle of the Big Hole

And then, as Natalekin neared a hollow where willows grew, suddenly three rifles cracked. The old man tumbled from his saddle.

Joseph leaped to his feet. More rifles cracked. The barking of Gatling guns was followed swiftly by shouts. Scarcely believing what his eyes told him, Joseph saw soldiers charging the upper end of the camp.

"Soldiers!" he shouted. "Soldiers right upon us!"

He reached for his gun and stumbled from his lodge. About him there was a terrible confusion. Warriors, heavy and slow with sleep, staggered from their lodges. Only a few thought to take their guns. All fled to the shelter of willows and alders along the bank of the stream at the lower end of camp.

Bullets peppered teepee walls. Bullets thudded against buffalo mats under which children stirred. Women ran from the lodges, herding children before them and sheltering babies in their arms.

"To the trees," Joseph shouted to his wife and daughter. "Hide there!"

He watched Toma Alwawinmy, her baby in her arms, run for the creek with Sound-of-Running-Feet. He saw them reach shelter and sink beneath the deep cold water to hide with the other women who were holding the heads of their little ones above the surface. Other women and children were not so fortunate. Joseph could not believe that the soldiers were shooting

121

at the women and children, but in the gray light of dawn, in the confusion of battle, bullets pelted everywhere.

Mothers caught out in the open fell dying. Other women snatched babies from dead mothers and carried the little ones to the doubtful safety of the creek. Lost children, frightened and confused, ran this way and that. Many children were killed before they could reach the shelter of the creek.

In the dreadful rout Chief Joseph tried to rally the men of his own band, tried to form them into battle line. White Bird, Looking Glass, and the war chiefs also shouted orders. A few warriors began shooting from what shelter they could find. But many had fled to the willows without their guns.

Joseph saw some that did not run from death. Shore Ice jumped into a small hollow, rolling a log in front of him to protect himself and his wife. He turned his gun on the advancing soldiers. A soldier shot Shore Ice. Joseph saw the wife seize the gun and shoot the soldier before she too fell with her body across her husband's.

So dies Shore Ice, Joseph thought. He started this war. Now it has killed him.

At the upper end of the camp, where soldiers first had attacked, flames now flared. A red torch of anger was

122

lit in Joseph's heart when he saw the smoke rise. The soldiers had fired the teepees.

"My brothers," he shouted in fury, "our homes are on fire! Get your guns! Fight! Why are you here?"

Above the noise of battle he could hear old White Bird roar, "Why are we retreating? Since the world was made, brave men have fought for their women and children. Shall we run to the mountains and let these white dogs kill our women and children? Fight! Shoot them down!"

The warriors rallied. Diving back through the gunfire to their teepees, they seized their guns. The chiefs called them together, shouted orders. The warriors fought now with fury. Close to their targets, they shot from all sides with deadly Nez Perce aim.

The horses! Joseph thought suddenly. Without horses the women and children could not escape.

Barefoot and without leggings, he led a band of braves in a mad dash up to a plateau where the frightened horses had run. There were white men there—not soldiers, but citizen volunteers.

"Attack them!" he ordered. "Get the horses!"

There was a fierce skirmish with the white men. But Joseph and his warriors reached the horses and drove them thundering back to camp. He turned the herd over to the women to keep behind the willows across the creek. Then he joined the braves, who were now fighting savagely to drive the soldiers from the camp.

Charge after rapid charge the Nez Perces thrust at the soldiers. Warriors darted from the willows to shoot at close range and then rushed back to shelter before the soldiers could even aim their guns. From both sides of the camp, from the hills above, Indian sharpshooters sent their bullets into the soldiers' line.

"They are caught in our crossfire," Joseph gloated to Ollocot who fought beside him.

The brothers watched the soldiers form two lines and fight back to back against the braves who charged from both sides of the camp.

"We grow too strong for them," Joseph said. "Now they will have to run."

The soldiers retreated across a stream and up to a plateau where a pine wood offered shelter. The Indians pressed on to attack, but the soldiers had dug rifle pits hastily and now fired from behind barricades.

"Leave them there," Joseph ordered. "They will be in a bad way up there. There is no water. They have no supplies with them. And our men can shoot from the hills above."

The Nez Perces swept back to their ruined camp. Chief Joseph saw the morning sun shine on the smoldering teepees and on the bodies of the dead. Thirty women and children had been killed and as many warriors. He wept. He saw other men strong in war weep as they hunted for the bodies of wives and children. Joseph knew that all hope of peace was now gone. From this time on every white man, soldier or settler, would be an enemy, for a mighty anger had been born in Nez Perce hearts. His people would be cold and hard and ruthless from now on.

"No time for grief," he told them. "We must bury the dead and tend the wounded. We must get the women and children safely away."

While teepee mats and buffalo robes and food were being packed, he questioned a captured soldier and learned that General Howard was approaching with more troops.

"It is General Howard we fear most," Joseph told White Bird. "We must get the women and children away."

It was afternoon before all was ready for the flight. The women and children, the boys and old men fled up the valley driving the horse herd before them. Chief Joseph and White Bird with a large party of warriors rode with the bands to protect the families. From now on the Nez Perces would keep the women and children safe. The wisest leaders hereafter would guard the families.

Thirty young warriors under the leadership of Ollocot and Looking Glass remained behind to hold the soldiers penned on their plateau. Joseph was worried, as he rode, about his brother. But he knew that Ollocot was a brave warrior; he must take his chances with death. His wife, Fair Land, had been wounded in the first attack, and Ollocot had hated to leave her even to the care of his brother. Joseph rode back down the line until he came to the travois on which Fair Land lay, her face white and drawn with pain.

"She will live?" he asked his wife, who rode beside the travois.

Toma Alwawinmy shook her head. "She will die. All this came too soon after her baby was born."

Chief Joseph rode sadly back to the head of the long line. The soldiers, he thought angrily, had much brutality to answer for today.

Southward he moved his people until he knew that they were well out of danger before he gave the orders to camp. At dawn some of the rear guard rode into camp, but Ollocot was not with them.

"Ollocot?" Joseph asked his cousin Yellow Wolf. "Does he live?"

"He lives. He and seven others stayed behind to watch the white men."

"Was there fighting?"

"Little fights. The soldiers tried to bring up a big gun on wheels. There was a pack mule with ammunition."

"You took the gun?"

126

Yellow Wolf nodded. "And the ammunition. Our hearts were glad then. We had bullets for our guns." He laughed. "The soldiers needed those bullets. They did not shoot much after that."

"Did you attack them?"

"A-aa, we had the bullets. We fought with those soldiers in their trenches. Red Moccasin Tops was badly wounded. Strong Eagle, his brother in war, went to help him."

Yellow Wolf told how Strong Eagle had inched down a shallow gulch to within twenty paces of the spot where his friend lay. Strong Eagle had sprung forward, raised his friend in his arms, and had begun a perilous run back to the Indian lines. Strong Eagle had been struck then—a bullet in his hip. But he had staggered almost to safety with his burden before he fell.

"Red Moccasin Tops died there," Yellow Wolf related. "But Strong Eagle crawled back to us. He is the only one of the Three Red Coats left, brothers in war who fought as one."

Yellow Wolf told how the thirty warriors had slid from tree to tree during the night, firing from different positions to make the soldiers think that a great horde of Indians surrounded the barricades. The soldiers, low on ammunition, had stopped firing.

"Many of us left then," Yellow Wolf said. "Only

127

Ollocot and six others stayed to keep watch on the soldiers."

Later that day Ollocot and his men caught up with the moving band. Joseph sighed with relief at seeing his brother. But there was sad news that must be told: Fair Land had died during the night of the first camp.

When Ollocot had recovered from his first hard grief, he told Joseph of the siege.

"At dawn," Ollocot said, "a white man came riding fast through the timber. Some wanted to kill him. But I said, 'No, let him go in. We will know what news he brings.' "

The rider had reached the trenches. A great cheer had gone up from the soldiers.

"I knew then that General Howard was near," Ollocot went on, "and we rode to join our people. We were needed here."

"That was good, my brother. We must fight now to protect our women and children from General Howard."

"I have no woman to protect," Ollocot said bitterly.

"You have a son," Joseph answered sternly. "You must keep the child safe."

12. ONLY MULES

CHIEF JOSEPH was concerned by the slow pace at which his people were forced to move south from the Big Hole Valley. They were hampered by the travois on which the many wounded must endure the jolting ride. The travois poles made snaky paths through the dust, leaving a trail that would be all too easy for General Howard to follow. The trail was marked also by the graves dug beside each night's camp for the wounded who had died during the day's travel.

Joseph had other worries. There was dissension among the Nez Perces. They had blamed Looking Glass for the losses at the Big Hole and had chosen a

129

new leader, Lean Elk, who knew all the trails in this new country they were entering.

"Lean Elk makes a good leader," Joseph told Ollo-cot.

"They should have chosen you."

"I am glad the people did not choose me. It is enough of a burden to keep the men of our own band from molesting the whites."

"They have memories of the Big Hole in their hearts," Ollocot said.

"A-aa, it is true. And the graves we dig each night keep hatred of the white man alive. It is hard to make my people obey the laws to protect the white settlers."

One day the Indians held up a pack train of eight wagons. The white teamsters, thinking to save their own lives, gave the young braves a keg of whiskey. The young men drank and the inevitable madness seized them. The freighters were killed, the wagons burned. Joseph and the other chiefs rode up and ordered the remaining whiskey poured on the ground before its evil fire could bring more trouble.

There were other killings of white settlers on lonely ranches. Cattle were stolen and slaughtered for food, and horses were appropriated wherever they were found. Chief Joseph was glad when Lean Elk turned the band through canyons to cross the Continental Divide back into eastern Idaho.

Only Mules

"We are out of Montana now," Joseph told his brother. "It was the people there that our young men hated for the Big Hole. Now we can keep our braves in order."

In the valley of the Lemhi River the chiefs made peace with the settlers, promising not to harm them in return for permission to pass southward through the valley.

The Nez Perces now kept scouts far to the rear of their line of march to watch for General Howard. The chiefs had learned a lesson at the Big Hole. They would not be surprised again.

And so Chief Joseph knew that the general and his troops were close behind. But the Nez Perces were three days in the lead, and they were heading rapidly enough toward the gap that would lift them through the mountains into Yellowstone Park. Once inside the park, Joseph felt that he could relax. Lean Elk knew many trails through that land of smoking pits and boiling geysers.

One morning after ten days of travel the tribe was encamped at the eastern end of a place called Camas Meadows. Yellowstone Park was only two days of riding ahead, Joseph knew. That morning he was watching preparations for the day's move when two scouts came riding fast into camp.

131

"Soldiers coming!" they reported to Joseph. "Soldiers not far back."

Hoping that this would not mean another battle, Chief Joseph sent out the call, "All warriors prepare for war!"

But by the time the fighting men had readied themselves for battle, another scout came galloping into camp.

"The soldiers have stopped fifteen miles back," he reported. "They are making camp. Some soldiers rode on ahead to the land of many smokes."

"No soldiers have passed this way," Chief Joseph said, puzzled.

"They rode round about. We watched but we could not see where they went."

"How many?" Joseph asked.

"Forty men."

The chiefs called a council and decided that the detachment of soldiers had been sent out to scout the Indian camp. In reality they had been sent ahead to bar the only pass into the Yellowstone.

"Let us make a surprise attack on Howard," suggested one of the younger war chiefs. "Forty of his men are gone. We can whip the rest of them."

"No," Joseph protested. "We do not want another battle. Besides, killing these men would do us no good. More soldiers would come. To fight would be like dig-

132

ging a hole in the sand. More sand always pours in to fill the hole."

Black Hair, a wounded warrior, had been unable to sleep the night before. A vision had come to him in the dark hours, and in the morning he had related his vision to some of the chiefs.

"I saw warriors," he had said, "riding back over the trail. It was dark. They took the soldiers' horses and left the white men afoot. I saw the warriors riding back to camp with many horses."

This vision was retold in council, and many of the chiefs decided that it was a good vision, foretelling success.

"We will not fight the soldiers," they said. "But let us take their horses. General Howard cannot follow us then."

Forty young warriors eagerly volunteered to attempt the mass stealing of horses. At sunset the forty warriors rode slowly toward the soldier camp.

"No talking," said Ollocot, who always led the young men. "No smoking. Do not strike a match."

He sent men ahead to steal in the darkness between the soldier outposts. They were to work silently as they cut the hobbles of the army pack animals and removed the bells from the lead mares.

"When the signal comes for attack," Ollocot told these advance men, "stampede the soldiers' mounts.

133

They graze free near the pack animals. We will get them all."

Ollocot and the rest of the warriors hid in the lava beds that surrounded the meadow to wait until the dark of the dawn. When Ollocot heard the long-drawn howl of a wolf, he knew that it was a signal that the scouts had done their work.

Through the dim light the warriors, divided into three parties, jogged toward the sentry. They were within fifty yards when a gun was fired accidentally at the rear of the Indian line. The plan of silence was spoiled.

Instantly Ollocot broke into loud war whoops, his men following suit. Galloping their horses, the Indians thundered down upon the camp. Wheeling, they circled the animal herd, firing and yelling. The Indian scouts dashed out of hiding. They rang the stolen bells of the lead mares wildly to make the horse herd follow. The camp was a nightmare of shots, galloping hoofs, of war whoops and bugle calls.

Away from the camp then swept Ollocot and his warriors, the herd pounding ahead of them. The soldiers had not even had time to get into their boots to answer the bugle. On the meadow the Indians headed north toward the lava rocks. The sun came up. And then the Nez Perces saw the prize they had captured.

134

Only Mules

"Ugh," Ollocot said in disgust. "Here are mules. Only mules."

Only three cavalry horses had been run off with the mules. Usually the soldiers let their mounts graze free during the night, but evidently this night they had carefully picketed their horses. The joke was on the raiders.

But they had little time to laugh at themselves. Behind them in the camp the bugle call of "Boots and Saddles" had been shrilling out. Now they looked back to see soldiers riding fast on fresh horses.

"To the rocks!" Ollocot shouted. "Take cover!"

He sent the mule herd galloping ahead with a few of his men. The others hastily scrambled up to the red ridges of rock on either side, ready to shoot down into the approaching line of soldiers. The soldiers, realizing that they were flanked, retreated.

But Indian scouts brought word that General Howard was now coming up with more soldiers and the big guns.

"No more fighting," Ollocot said. "We will get out of here. We are too few. And we have the mules."

Driving their booty of one hundred and fifty mules before them, the Indians rode back to camp, shame-faced.

When Chief Joseph saw the mules, he laughed and

said, "We will have plenty of pack animals now. And General Howard will have none."

The Nez Perces loaded the new pack animals and moved on in a leisurely way toward the pass into the Yellowstone. They had plenty of time now.

In the meantime the general moved his camp to Henry's Lake in eastern Idaho to wait until he could replace his mules. His men also needed food supplies and winter clothing before he could march them into the cold altitudes of the park. He hoped that Lieutenant Bacon, who commanded the detachment sent ahead to the pass, could hold the Indians until the greater force could catch up.

The lieutenant had reached the western entrance to Yellowstone. There he waited two days without seeing any sign of Indians. He decided that they must have preceded him across the pass and ordered his men back over the trail to join Howard.

When Joseph and his people reached the pass after their delayed march, they rode into Yellowstone without a soldier to stop them.

136

13. YELLOWSTONE PARK

ONE MORNING in the park they were encamped on the Firehole River. Chief Joseph was startled to hear shouts followed by rifle shots. Hurrying toward the sound of the disturbance, he found a group of young braves gleefully tearing to pieces a bright new buggy. Some were brandishing the yellow spokes of the wheels and boasting that the spokes would make fine whip handles. To one side of the buggy Yellow Wolf was doing his best to keep other braves from a white man, a woman, and a young girl. Joseph saw at once that the lives of white people were in danger and he hurried to protect them.

"What is this that you do?" he asked the braves angrily. "We want no more white blood spilled." The

137

young braves slunk away, growling. Joseph turned to Yellow Wolf. "Who are these whites?"

"They were camped by one of the boiling waters. We took them prisoners. The braves saw us coming and rode out to meet us. There were four other white men but—"

"What happened to the others?" Joseph interrupted.

"They jumped into the bushes, trying to escape. One was shot. The others escaped."

Chief Joseph turned away for a moment in disgust at the actions of his young men. But Yellow Wolf was not to blame.

"You have done well, my cousin," Joseph told the youth. "Come, we will take them to my lodge. There they will be safe."

There would have to be a council of the chiefs, he knew. Only the council could decide what to do with these prisoners. In the meantime he would take them under his guard.

Through an interpreter he talked to the young white man, who said he was Frank Carpenter of Radersburg, Montana. The woman was his sister, Mrs. George Cowan, and the girl was his younger sister Ida.

"We thought it would be great sport to drive through Yellowstone. It's just been made a national park, you know. We were camped at the edge of the Lower Geyser Basin—our last night in the park. This morning your Indians surprised us. Some of them seemed friendly. This one that you call Yellow Wolf even shook hands with me."

Chief Joseph smiled. That was why Yellow Wolf had tried to save the white people. Once he had given his hand in friendship, he would try to keep this young man from harm. Joseph turned to his cousin.

"Why did you bring the white people to camp?" he asked.

"The young man wanted to see you. He said he had heard of the great Chief Joseph."

Joseph sighed. He knew that General Howard and all the whites considered him the head chief of the warring Nez Perce bands. For all that his people did that was evil he was blamed. For all that was good he was praised. Friendly Montana ranchers had told him that the white man's newspapers claimed that this was his war and that he was the great leader of his people. And yet he was only one of many chiefs. He did not want the kind of fame the white men were giving him.

Leaving the prisoners with Toma Alwawinmy, Joseph called the other chiefs to a council. None of them wanted more trouble, but they feared to set the white people free. The Nez Perces did not want General Howard to know where they were in the Park. The council decided that the whites must be kept as prisoners for a few days.

139

That night Emma Cowan, who thought her husband was the man shot in the squabble with the braves, wept for him. To console herself she took Chief Joseph's baby on her lap. Joseph smiled briefly, but Toma Alwawinmy laughed with joy as she watched the white stranger play with her baby. The Indian woman saw the tears on Emma Cowan's face and turned to young Carpenter.

"She weeps. Why?" Toma Alwawinmy asked in English, for she had gone to the mission school and could speak the white man's language.

"She thinks her husband was killed today," the young man answered.

"Her heart weeps. I am sorry," the Indian woman said softly.

The next morning Emma Cowan and the frightened, pretty Ida were mounted behind reliable warriors for the day's ride. Carpenter was ordered to walk and to help the Indian women carry water for the noon meal and unpack at night.

Three days later after the Nez Perces had crossed the Yellowstone River, the chiefs decided the fate of their captives.

"We will free you to go to your homes," Chief Joseph told the prisoners that night in his lodge.

He gave the women food and horses but told Carpenter that he must walk. Lean Elk took the little party secretly across the river and pointed out a trail to them.

"That is the way," Lean Elk said. "Ride all night. Do not sleep. Ride all day. You are not safe from our young men. Hurry."

The sisters and brother traveled through the forest and came out of the park at last at Mammoth Hot Springs. Here they found a troop of soldiers scouting for the Nez Perce trail. Mrs. Cowan learned that her husband had not been killed after all. He had escaped and was waiting for her at a nearby ranch.

Relieved that the white people had been freed, Chief Joseph rode with his tribe around Yellowstone Lake, leaving the park by a trail up Pelican Creek to the Montana Absaroka Mountains. Scouts brought daily word that General Howard and his troops were floundering behind through the maze of mountains, canyons, and forests.

Chief Joseph had been looking forward to reaching Montana, for he remembered his happy hunting trip there as a boy. His band had visited then with the friendly Crow Indians. The Crows, he felt sure, would now help his people against General Howard. They would welcome the Nez Perces and ask them to stay in the buffalo country.

But Joseph was bitterly disappointed. The Crows,

141

fearful of the power of the soldiers, refused to help. Sadly he decided that there was no way for his people to find peace except by riding on to Canada. He knew that Chief Sitting Bull of the Sioux Indians had left the United States and found freedom in Canada. Joseph had heard that Sitting Bull once said, "God made me an Indian, but he did not make me a reservation Indian." Sitting Bull and he would have much in common.

One day scouts brought Joseph word that a troop of three hundred and fifty soldiers under Colonel Sturgis had been sent out from the Montana Tongue River Military Station to intercept the Indians.

"They lost themselves in the mountains," the scouts said, grinning. "They ended up by finding General Howard. But they did not find us."

Chief Joseph smiled at the thought of this lost army, but he was worried just the same. Now there were two armies following his people, although both were still a safe distance behind.

He was glad when they crossed the Yellowstone River at Laurel, Montana, and turned down the north bank a short way. Ahead of his tribe now lay endless tableland. It was dry country, but there was bunch grass for the horses and there were rivers to provide drinking water. The going would be easier now, Joseph thought.

Not far down the river his young men captured a

stagecoach. Passengers and driver fled to the shelter of the willows. The warriors had so much fun with the stagecoach that they let the white people go unharmed. Joseph smiled as he watched his braves take turns driving and riding in the stage, whipping up the horses to full speed, yelling in glee over their bumpy ride. There had been little enough joy on this long march, he thought. Let the young men have their fun.

But all at once came the familiar shout, "Soldiers coming!"

On the trail behind the stagecoach Joseph saw many blue-coated riders. Sturgis and his men had found the Nez Perces. Joseph did not wait to see the stagecoach fun abandoned. His warriors were well trained. He knew that they would scramble for their horses and guns. Turning his mount, he galloped fast to the camp, for he had been assigned the duty of seeing that the women and children were kept safe.

"Pack up," he ordered the women. "Escape away. Up that canyon there."

Up a flat valley toward an opening in the canyon walls the women fled. Joseph soon saw soldiers galloping toward them to cut off the retreat. With Chief White Bird and a band of warriors he rode out to hold the flat while the women and children rode to safety behind him. Soon the other fighting men of the tribe

143

joined Joseph, and all retreated toward the canyon. The soldiers pursued to find themselves flanked by Indian sharpshooters manning the rocks above. There was fierce fighting for a time, but the soldiers withdrew at nightfall.

All night Chief Joseph kept his people scurrying up the canyon. For two days soldiers were close at their heels. But by the time the Nez Perces had reached the Musselshell River, Sturgis and his soldiers were out of sight.

"He has given up," Joseph told White Bird. "We rode too fast for him."

But now the scouts reported that General Howard had come up by a different route and was not far behind. Scouts watched each day and reported the distance between Indian forces and white.

"We are safe enough," the chiefs said. "When Howard moves slowly, we can slow up. When he is catching up, we will go faster. We will keep two days ahead of him."

What Joseph and the other chiefs did not know was that General Howard had made a clever plan. He had noticed that the warring bands always slowed their pace to match his. And he had sent a messenger ahead to Colonel Miles, who was stationed at Tongue River. Miles was to take all the soldiers at his disposal and

144

march north by a shorter route to intercept the Nez Perces. Howard would loiter along behind the Indians to keep them moving slowly. This lingering would give Miles time to head off the Nez Perces before they could cross the Missouri River.

Nez Perce scouts watched only Howard and Sturgis. They did not know that Colonel Miles had set out with a force of six hundred men—cavalry, infantry, scouts, and Cheyenne Indian guides. Miles was riding toward the Missouri at the mouth of the Musselshell.

The unsuspecting Joseph was glad when General Howard slowed his march. It was good that the people could make long camps to allow the wounded to recover and to rest the horses.

Happy to be leisurely, he rode on with his people. They were heading for the Cow Island crossing of the Missouri, about halfway between Fort Benton and Fort Peck, Montana. There was shallow water at Cow Island, the last point on the Missouri that steamers could reach in the dry fall months. Food and supplies were brought up the river by boat and then freighted overland to the Canadian Mounted Police. Small boats took the freight farther up the river to Helena, Montana, and Fort Benton.

When Chief Joseph rode up to the Cow Island crossing with the families he was guarding, he saw a large pile of freight dumped on the shore. A steamer had just unloaded, and he could see it puffing back down the river. There were army tents across the river, and he knew that soldiers would be stationed there to guard the freight. When they came out of their tents, he counted them. Only twelve soldiers. They would be no threat to his people. But just to be safe he ordered twenty warriors to cross the river first.

"Stay between the women and children and the guns of the soldiers," he ordered. "If they do not fire on you, we will do no shooting."

The soldiers took one look at the long line of warriors and barricaded themselves in a little fort, leaving the freight piled high on the river bank. There would be food supplies in that freight, Joseph knew.

"Two men carry a white flag to the soldiers," he ordered. "Ask them if they will sell us food."

The soldiers refused. The warriors surrounded the fort to hold the soldiers behind the barricade. The Indian women helped themselves to the food in the freight dump—flour, sugar, coffee, bacon. Chief Joseph allowed the pilfering. Although his people were breaking a Nez Perce law, he felt that he was in the right. He had offered to pay and had been refused. Besides, this was war, and his people were hungry.

The officer in charge at Cow Island sent a dispatch

146

to Fort Benton that night. With true sagebrush wit he wrote:

Colonel:
   Chief Joseph is here, and says he will surrender for two hundred pounds of sugar. I told him to surrender without the sugar. He took the sugar and will not surrender. What will I do?

14. "I WILL FIGHT NO MORE"

A<small>FTER</small> the crossing of the Missouri, the Nez Perces voted to take the leadership away from Lean Elk and to give it back to Looking Glass. That easygoing chief had complained that Lean Elk was pushing the people too hard. General Howard was now six days behind.

"Why hurry?" Looking Glass said.

Slowly, making long and restful camps, the Nez Perces moved toward the Canadian border. They were heading for the Bearpaw Mountains.

Chief Joseph grieved because his people were weary. And it was no wonder, he thought, for they had covered over fifteen hundred miles of rough country.

The soldiers pursuing them so relentlessly had carried only necessary supplies. His people had been burdened with what remained of the possessions of a lifetime. Their marches had been hampered by four hundred women and many children, by the old and the sick.

His people were not only tired, but suffering. The wounded, tortured by the long march, were not recovering. Food supplies were growing short, and there were few buffalo robes to keep his people warm in the nights already cold. Icy winds from the mountains foretold the blizzards that soon would come swirling down. He was glad for the long rests that would keep the tribe going, but he felt again that disturbing sense of danger near.

What he could not know was that Colonel Miles also had crossed the Missouri with his six hundred soldiers. Miles was making long forced marches in a diagonal across the country straight toward the Bearpaw Mountains.

It was the end of September when Joseph and his people reached the northern slope of the Bearpaws. Canada and freedom were only two sun's march away.

The teepees were set up in a sheltered valley along the banks of Snake Creek. It was a good camp, Joseph thought. High bluffs rose to the south and east. The valley was cut by two coulees, deep enough to give protection in case of battle. Scouts riding ahead had killed buffalo, and the meat was waiting to give strength to his weary people. There was no wood for fires, but there were buffalo chips. The women could cook.

"I sat down in a fat and beautiful land," Chief Joseph said afterwards. "I had won my freedom and the freedom of my people. There were many empty places in the lodges and in the council, but we were in a land where we would not be forced to live in a place we did not want."

He was not eager to leave the United States. He still believed that if he could stay safe at a distance and talk straight to the men who would be sent him by the President, he would be able to persuade the government to allow his people to return to Wallowa.

The next morning the camp made leisurely preparations to move on. Breakfast was cooked, and a few families already were packed. Many of the women had gone to the meadow where the horses grazed, to bring the pack animals to camp.

Suddenly two youths who had been out for a hunt came galloping in from the north.

"Buffaloes stampeding!" they shouted. "They run from something. Maybe soldiers coming!"

Joseph was alarmed, but Looking Glass saw no need for hurry. Why should trouble come from the north? There were no soldiers there.

151

"Take plenty time," he called out to the people. "Let the children eat all they want. There is no hurry."

The packing went slowly on. But an hour later Chief Joseph looked up to the bluffs to see an Indian rider running his horse at full speed along the rim. At the highest point he stopped and waved the blanket signal that meant, "Soldiers coming! Soldiers right upon us!"

Warriors seized guns and cartridge belts, mounted their horses and galloped off toward the bluffs. The camp was now in turmoil—women struggling with packs, children running about screaming those words that summer-long had been the Nez Perce call to battle, "Soldiers coming! Soldiers!"

Chief Joseph leaped out into the open.

"The horses!" he shouted. "We must get the horses!"

He ran to the meadow where fifty to a hundred horses stood waiting, packs lashed to their backs. There was no time to get the horses back to the camp.

"Run!" he ordered the women and children who worked at the packing. "Take horses that are not saddled. Ride. Fifty warriors go with the women and children for a guard."

He looked up to see soldiers already galloping in two wide circling wings down upon the camp. The right wing swept past the lodges and on toward the horse herd. Chief Joseph saw the danger coming. To his little daughter Sound-of-Running-Feet he threw a rope.

152

"I Will Fight No More"

"Catch a horse," he ordered her. "Join the others. Escape with those on horseback."

Sound-of-Running-Feet obeyed. Joseph watched her ride off with the others. He did not know that he was never to see this daughter again. Soon the escaping band was cut off from the camp by the soldiers who had run off a thousand horses.

Now he saw his own danger. The soldiers had him blocked from the lodges. He thought of Toma Alwawinmy and his four-month-old baby girl surrounded by soldiers. He would go to them or die.

Unmindful of bullets, he dashed through the line of soldiers. There were guns on every side, before and behind him. His clothes were cut to pieces, his horse was wounded. But he was not hurt.

He reached the door of his lodge. Toma Alwawinmy handed him his rifle.

"Here is your gun," she said. "Fight."

He joined the warriors who were holding off the soldiers in front of the lodges. He saw the blue line of fast-riding cavalry men sweeping down upon the Indian line. For a minute he thought his warriors would crumble.

"We die here," he called out to them. "Do not give your lives cheaply. Shoot the leader, not the soldier."

After that his warriors shot, cool and sure, with

153

deadly aim. Every time an officer lifted his voice in a word of command, a bullet found him.

Only minutes after that first sweeping charge of the six hundred soldiers on the camp, Chief Joseph heard the army bugles sound a withdrawal.

But the soldiers withdrew only to lay siege to the camp. All day the battle went on. A band of warriors fought on the butte above the camp, driving the soldiers back with steady firing. Chief Joseph and the remaining warriors were hammered back, to fight from the two dry coulees behind the camp.

Late in the afternoon the soldiers charged the camp again—this time to try to cut the Indians off from water. The fighting grew heavier, and Joseph saw many of his men killed, for the soldiers had big guns. But again Nez Perce firing was too much for the soldiers and they were forced back. Wounded soldiers lay close to the Indian line without water.

"Do not kill the soldiers," Joseph ordered. "Carry water to them instead."

Night came down, black and cold. An icy wind swept down from the north. Snow swirled through heavy air.

"No more fighting tonight," Chief Joseph told the men near him. "The guns will stop. We can rest and count our dead."

When he came to the camp, he drank the first water

154

since morning. But when he learned how many leaders, how many brave warriors his people had lost, he did not want food. Toohulhulzote had been killed. Strong Eagle, the last of the Three Red Coats, had died fighting fiercely.

And when Chief Joseph passed the lodge of Ollocot, he heard the women wailing the Death Chant and knew that his brother had been killed. Ollocot, who had been like a third hand. Ollocot, who had led the young men. Ollocot, his loved brother.

Joseph's heart felt choked and heavy, but there was no time for grief. There was work to do. Hemmed in on all sides by soldiers, all hope of escape was gone. His people had few horses left. The fighting must be finished here on this flat. He must see that his people spent the night in preparation for tomorrow's battle.

"Dig trenches," he told them. "Rifle pits for the warriors up on the butte. Shelter pits for the women and children here in the camp."

Both men and women dug with any tools they could find—the sharpened edges of frying pans, shovels, the curved sticks used for uprooting camas bulbs. There could be no lights for fear of drawing the soldiers' bullets, no warming fires, no hot food for the children. Toward dawn Joseph had the satisfaction of seeing the children rolled in buffalo robes and hidden deep and safe in the completed underground shelters.

Thunder Rolling

Morning came. The battle began again. The besieged camp was battered with bullets. The big guns had been brought close by the soldiers, and now shells exploded among the lodges and over the pits. The wild wind brought the blizzard down from the north, hard pellets swirling in a dance of death.

Fighting tirelessly with his warriors, Joseph knew in his heart that this was his last battle for Nez Perce freedom. Through all that day's sorrow thoughts came to him of his beloved Land of the Winding Waters— memories of white teepees standing in peace beside the lake, memories of the curling smoke of home fires rising toward the sheltering mountains. Far away behind the curtain of the drifting snows he saw his homeland.

On the morning of the third day of battle, the firing went on although the blizzard still raged. But Chief Joseph saw that neither side was taking much hurt. Red men and white shot from sheltering rifle pits, but bullets seldom found a mark through the curtaining snow.

But on that morning word was brought to Joseph that Chief Looking Glass had been killed. He had stood up at the edge of his pit to see better, and the bullet of a soldier sharpshooter had found his heart. Joseph knew that he must now take over the lead of all three Nez Perce bands. He was the only chief left to lead in battle, for White Bird was too old for fighting.

156

"I Will Fight No More"

In the afternoon of that day Joseph saw a white flag
go up above the soldier line.

"Colonel Miles would like to talk to Chief Joseph,"
a voice called out in English.

Chief Joseph called a council at once. "I will go,"
he offered. "We will see what the white men have to
say."

Perhaps he had some dim hope of taking his people
back to their own country. For always he had believed
that if he would say the right words, the white men
would listen. At any rate, he sent his interpreter into
the soldiers' camp to carry a message of willingness to
talk.

After a time, while Joseph waited watching and
hoping, the interpreter and Colonel Miles with a few
soldiers walked to a halfway point between the lines.
The interpreter motioned for Joseph to join the group
under the white flag.

Chief Joseph had no reason to trust a flag of truce.
For a moment he hesitated, remembering how his peace
sign had been answered at the beginning of the White
Bird Battle. But if there was any chance that the white
men really wanted peace, he must risk his life. With
dignity he walked to meet Colonel Miles.

Miles shook hands in a friendly way. "Come," he
said, "let us go and sit by my fire and talk this matter
over."

157

Thunder Rolling

The white chief seemed to be sincere in his welcome, Joseph thought. He walked with the soldiers to a tent where there was a warm fire. They talked for a time of peace terms. Joseph was so encouraged that he even agreed to give up his gun and those of the few warriors who had accompanied him. But no sooner was this done than he caught sly remarks in English that did not sound like peace. At once he turned and started back toward his camp.

There was a scuffle. The unarmed Joseph and his warriors were taken prisoner. A mighty anger filled his heart. The white flag of truce had been only another lie—a trick to take him prisoner. Now his people would be without a leader. At least Miles allowed the other warriors to return to the Indian camp.

"Tell my people," Joseph said, "that the white men do not want peace. The fighting is not over."

Toward evening a war chief, Yellow Bull, risked capture to ask permission to talk to his beloved chief. The two were not allowed to be alone, but they talked together as if no soldiers were there.

"They have you now," Yellow Bull said. "I am afraid they will never let you go. But we have an officer in our camp, a man named Jerome. We took him prisoner. We will hold him as a hostage until they let you go free."

"That is good," Chief Joseph said. "But if they kill

158

me, do not kill the white man. Killing will do our people no good."

But that night Joseph's anger rose to white heat when the soldiers treated him with indignities that no chief should be asked to endure. His hands and feet were tied. He was hobbled like a horse. What was more insulting, he was rolled, like a papoose in a cradle-board, into a buffalo robe. And then he was put into a shelter to sleep with the army mules.

The next day soldiers came to untie him. Still smarting under the shame he had suffered, he was taken to a central spot between the lines. The Nez Perces brought the white officer, and the two prisoners were exchanged.

"We must fight on," Chief Joseph told his people when he was back in his own lines. "The white men are not ready for peace. The war is not over."

To Yellow Bull he said, "What did you do to the white officer Jerome?"

"We gave him food and water, blankets to keep him warm. We let him walk back and forth as he wished."

"I was not treated that way," Joseph said, smiling grimly. "I was made to sleep with mules."

For three more days the fight dragged on, each side taking pot shots at each other through the wind-driven fury of the snow. Once Joseph saw a herd of buffalo, running before the storm. For a moment they loomed, only to vanish into the gray wall that was the prairie. If the Nez Perces were only free to hunt the buffalo, he thought. His people were starving in the shelter pits. He could hear the children wailing with hunger and the bitter cold. The women dared not leave the pits, but had to sleep sitting upright. His people could not last out this siege much longer.

At noon on October fifth, he saw two Indians carrying a white flag of truce toward his lines.

"Wait," he ordered his warriors. "Hold your fire. They are Nez Perces."

As the men came nearer, Joseph recognized one of them as a Mission Nez Perce known as Captain John, who often acted as an interpreter for the white men. He had a married daughter in the besieged camp.

"My brothers," Captain John called out, "I am glad to see you alive today. Colonel Miles wants to make friends with Chief Joseph today. There will be no more war."

But Joseph, remembering his last experience under a flag of truce, was not willing to listen. He sent the messengers back to the soldier lines. Later in the day they came again.

"General Howard has come up," they told Joseph. "There are now too many soldiers for you. A thousand soldiers, and you have only a few living. General Howard wishes to talk with you. Colonel Miles says

that if you will surrender, he will let you go back to
your homes. He will take you to a safe place this
winter. In the spring you can go home. He promises
this."

A thousand soldiers, Joseph thought bitterly. And
his people had less than seventy left to fight. Besides,
to go back to Wallowa—that was the hope of his heart,
what he had been fighting for. This was the promise he
had waited to hear. With faith in this promise, he
agreed to surrender.

Late that afternoon Captain John took Joseph's
answer back to Colonel Miles and General Howard.
The sun fought with the storm as the old Indian rode
up the hill.

Two hours later, toward sunset, Chief Joseph rode
slowly, sadly up the same hill. He bowed his head in
sorrow as he listened to the quiet words of four warrior
friends who walked beside his horse. Surrender was not
easy for a chief who had been proud and free.

He laid the rifle that he must surrender across the
saddle in front of him and clasped his hands on his
pommel. He knew that he did not look the part of a
great chief. His buckskin clothing was worn and tattered. His wrists and head were marked by the slashes
of raking bullet wounds. The eagle feathers had long
since been shot from his hair, and his black braids

161

hung rough and heavy. He knew that his face must show the bitter grief of his defeat.

When he neared the officers, he straightened his shoulders. Dismounting, he handed the reins to one of his warriors. For a long sad moment he looked at his friends, but he could speak no word of comfort. Then he drew his gray blanket closer about him and turned away to walk toward the two waiting officers.

There was hatred in his heart as he offered his rifle to General Howard with a slow dignified gesture of the arm. Here was the man who had forced the Nez Perces from their home. Here was the stern general who had followed them so relentlessly, the officer who had caused the death of so many loved ones.

General Howard indicated that Joseph was to hand his rifle to Colonel Miles. The chief did so. Then, stepping back a pace, Chief Joseph spoke in Nez Perce the simple, tragic words of his surrender.

"Tell General Howard I know his heart. What he told me before I have in my heart. I am tired of fighting. Our chiefs are killed. Looking Glass is dead. Toohulhulzote is dead. The old men are dead. It is the young who say yes or no. He who led the young men is dead. It is cold and we have no blankets. The little children are freezing to death. My people, some of them, have run away to the hills and have no blankets, no food; no one knows where they are—perhaps freezing to

162

death. I want to have time to look for my children and see how many I can find. Maybe I shall find them among the dead.

"Hear me, my chiefs, I am tired. My heart is sick and sad. From where the sun now stands, I will fight no more forever."

Both officers shook hands with the chief, and Joseph took each proffered hand. Then he turned silently away and walked with dignity to the tent that was to be his prison.

Behind him in the Nez Perce camp he knew that his people were lifting hands toward the sky where the sun cut dimly through the storm clouds.

"No more war," he heard them shout. "No more fighting."

And Chief Joseph, the man of peace, was comforted. He had surrendered, but his people no longer would have to suffer hunger, weariness, and death.

15. "LET ME BE A FREE MAN"

Aʟʟ ᴛʜᴀᴛ ᴇᴠᴇɴɪɴɢ Chief Joseph watched with pity while his worn and tattered men straggled into the army camp to give up their guns. He was sad of heart, but he was relieved when he was told that hot food had been sent to the Indian camp to warm Nez Perce children from the bitter wind. He thought of his own daughter, out in the storm, lost somewhere in a strange land.

He turned to Lieutenant C. E. S. Wood, who had been assigned to attend the captive chief. Joseph liked this kind young man. In fact, the two began that night a friendship that was to last for many years.

"When my young cousin Yellow Wolf comes to

give up his gun, I would like to talk with him. Could I?"

"I will see that he comes here," Wood promised.

When Yellow Wolf arrived, Joseph told the young brave, "Your mother escaped that first morning of the fighting. I do not know if she caught a horse or was afoot. Go and find her. Find Sound-of-Running-Feet, my daughter. Bring her to me."

Yellow Wolf slipped through the soldier guards and caught a stray horse. He rode away, searching in the fallen snow for the track of the escaped women. The blizzard had buried all traces of the trail, but later he found the starving women. He did not return Sound-of-Running-Feet to her father. Freedom was too sweet. Instead he rode on with a roving band to find refuge among the Sioux Indians of Sitting Bull in Canada. A year passed before ˏhe was able to take Joseph's daughter to the Nez Perce Reservation at Lapwai.

Chief Joseph mourned his daughter as dead. He was alone now except for his baby girl. Toma Alwawinmy had been killed during the last hours of the battle.

He learned that many had escaped in the dark of that first night of captivity. Chief White Bird and most of his men, refusing to surrender, had slipped through the soldier picket line to ride off to Canada. With a touch of bitterness Joseph remembered that it was White Bird's young men who had started the war with the Salmon River murders. Yet the old chief would

166

ride free, while the chief who was blameless would remain a prisoner.

Four hundred and eighteen Nez Perces, most of them women, children, and old men, followed the lead of Joseph and surrendered. Only forty warriors gave up their guns. The others had been killed in the battle or had escaped afterwards. The remnants of the horse herd, gaunt and half-starved, was turned over to the soldiers. A hundred saddles were given up.

His people were poor indeed now, Chief Joseph thought as he rode with them to Fort Keogh, near what is now Miles City, Montana.

"You will winter on the Yellowstone River," Colonel Miles told Joseph. "But in the spring you and your people will be returned to Idaho as soon as the mountain trails are clear of snow. You will, of course, have to go on the reservation."

With this promise Joseph had to be content. He knew that he would not be allowed to return to Wallowa, but on the reservation he would be near. Above him would be the blue skies that he loved, and perhaps sometime he would be allowed to see once more his own beloved valley.

He could not help thinking bitterly that if the Nez Perces had gone on the reservation when he had urged them, many would not now be dead and others scattered through the mountains of a strange land. And

167

these who shared his captivity would not now be without horses and guns, without lands of their own. But captive or free, he still was chief. He would lead his people as best he could.

"General Howard has gone to the East to talk to General Phil Sheridan about you," Colonel Miles told Joseph when the Indians were encamped on the Yellowstone. "General Howard will see to it that the terms of the treaty are kept."

"A-aa, it is good. We will wait," Joseph said.

But one day Colonel Miles came to Joseph in a temper. General Sheridan would not agree that the promises made to Joseph be kept.

"I am ordered to move you and your band on to Bismark, South Dakota. General Sheridan says that your people can be fed more easily there."

Eight hundred miles more Chief Joseph traveled with his weary people. Half of the men and many of the women had been wounded. All, especially the children, were worn and thin from the long riding and the many battles.

Colonel Miles, angry because he felt sure that his pledge to Joseph was going to be broken, did his best to make the Indians comfortable for the journey. Joseph watched the women and children, the sick and wounded loaded on flatboats to be carried down the river in ease. He and the able-bodied warriors rode overland with Colonel Miles and the Seventh Cavalry. River and land parties reached Bismark at the same time.

Chief Joseph was surprised to find the little town buzzing with welcoming excitement. He was met by a brass band and an escort from the fort. Citizens pressed gifts of food upon his people. He could not understand why prisoners of war should be treated with such honors.

"Why do they welcome us?" he asked Miles.

The colonel smiled. "They have heard about the great Chief Joseph. They admire you and your people. The citizens are having a big banquet, and you are to be guest of honor."

Joseph received this written invitation:

To Joseph, Head Chief of the Nez Perces:
Sir:—Desiring to show you our kind feelings and the admiration we have for your bravery and humanity, as exhibited in your recent conflict with the forces of the United States, we most cordially invite you to dine with us at the Sheridan House in this city. The dinner to be given at 1½ P.M. today.

At the banquet the puzzled chief was told that he might order what he wanted to eat. The ways of the white men were strange, he thought.

"Can we have salmon?" he asked.

The salmon was brought. Pleased, he ate with appetite.

"The food is good," he said. "This salmon reminds me of my own country."

After the banquet Colonel Miles had bad news for Joseph.

"You and your people are to be moved on to Fort Leavenworth, Kansas. I fear this means that you will not be sent back to Idaho next Spring."

"We were promised," Joseph said, so stunned that he could think of no other words to say.

"I know. I have done all I could. I wrote to the Secretary of War. I told him you were the most intelligent Indian I had ever met. I told him how you counseled against war. I told him how your people had been wronged. General Howard has been working for you also."

"I do not blame you and General Howard. I know you would not break a promise. But I do not understand."

"The Secretary of War," Miles explained dryly, "says he is afraid that if you go back there will be more fighting. The friends and relatives of the murdered whites on the Salmon River are threatening trouble for you."

"I did not have anything to do with those murders," Joseph answered mildly. "I was not there."

He was bewildered. How could the United States Government refuse to honor the terms of the surrender? Nez Perce law taught, "Never break a promise." He had given up to the Army his guns and saddles and eleven hundred fine Nez Perce horses. Never would he have surrendered without the promise of return to Idaho. Now the government had broken that promise.

His bewilderment turned to indignation, but all he said was, "Somebody has got our horses."

Joseph and his people rode the train to their next camp on the lowlands of the Missouri River. He hated the Kansas camp because it was harmful to his people. The water was warm and unhealthful to drink. Malaria rose in the mists at night to attack the aged, the wounded, and the children so thin from their endless journeying.

"My heart suffered for my people," Joseph protested afterward. "The Great Spirit who rules above seemed to be looking the other way, and did not see what was being done to my people."

But Joseph was to suffer even more for his people. When the warm spring weather came, the Nez Perces that had survived the winter were moved to the Oklahoma Indian Territory. *Eeikish Pah,* they called it with loathing—That Hot Place. Chief Joseph had to watch two hundred and sixty of his people shake with the chills and fever of the malaria contracted in Kansas. Many of the old, those wounded in the war, and the little children died. Few of the newborn babies lived.

Joseph's little baby, born just before the White Bird Battle, died of the fever. The lines of sadness on the chief's face deepened until they made channels between his nostrils and the corners of his grim mouth.

He was not entirely alone now, however. Nez Perces for years had practiced polygamy, since there were many more women than men in the band. He had taken the two wives of Chief Looking Glass into his lodge. Such marriages were a customary courtesy among the Nez Perces. The wives of a brave chief killed in battle must not be left uncared for. Perhaps he learned then, with two women in his lodge, that wives could have minds of their own when it came to the management of household affairs. Years later he said, "When you can get the last word with an echo, you may have the last word with your wife."

Chief Joseph rode with the Commissioner of Indian Affairs, E. A. Hayt, to choose land in the Indian Territory. In his report Hayt said that Joseph was "gentlemanly and well-behaved . . . bright and intelligent . . . anxious for the welfare of his people." Hayt recommended that the Nez Perces, whom he considered a

172

superior people, should be put on land "where they would thrive."

Joseph asked for lands on the Ponca Reservation, but his people were placed instead on a piece of low, unhealthful ground. He protested. Finally he was given permission to go to Washington to plead the cause of his people before President Hayes.

While the chief was in the city, he gave an interview which told the sufferings of his people and the story of his own life. This interview was published in the *North American Review* in April, 1879. In this translated talk he showed his grasp of the problem of the Indian. He said:

> I know that my race must change. We cannot hold our own with the white men as we are. We only ask an even chance to live as other men live. We ask to be recognized as men. We ask that the same law shall work alike on all men.

He expressed his dream of life for his people:

> Whenever the White man treats the Indians as they treat each other, then we shall have no more wars. We shall be all alike—brothers of one father and one mother, with one sky above us and one country around us, and one government for all. . . . For this time the Indian race is waiting and praying.

Thunder Rolling

A part of this published talk voiced the appeal of all the oppressed people of the world—yesterday and today:

> Let me be a free man—free to travel, free to stop, free to trade where I choose, free to choose my own teachers, free to follow the religion of my fathers, free to think and talk and act for myself— and I will obey every law, or submit to the penalty.

16. ALMOST HOME AGAIN

Chief Joseph was not allowed to lead his people back to the West in the spring. But he was given over ninety thousand acres of the land on the Ponca Reservation for which he had asked.

"It is land you do not want," he told his people. "But it is good land, and we must work hard on it. We must show the Great White Father in Washington that our hearts are good."

He kept them working until they raised all their own vegetables and some grain. But his people were natural herders, not gardeners. And so when the government gave the tribe a hundred head of cattle and some horses, the herds increased greatly.

Chief Joseph saw to it that his people made no trouble for the Indian Agent. When a school was provided, he urged all children to attend.

"If we must live in the white man's world," he said, "you must learn the white man's ways."

But in spite of his labors Chief Joseph was not happy. He was homesick for the West, for the glory of soaring mountain against living sky. He thirsted for one drink of clear, cold mountain water. He longed for one breath of mountain air, fragrant with the tang of pine and sage.

Seven years went by. Time paced slowly for him during those years, but he never gave up his efforts to have his people returned to the West. Again and again he made appeals. He knew that others were working for him also. Miles, a general now, did what he could. Other white friends, aroused to sympathy by the story told in the magazine article, were working for the Nez Perces.

There were times when Chief Joseph felt hopeless. Daily he grieved as he watched his people sicken and die of the humid air and the low altitude. With dread he noticed that few babies were now born among his people. The tribe would soon die out unless he could take his people back to the West.

At last the orders came from the government. Chief Joseph was overjoyed, but his joy was tinged with sadness. One hundred and fifty deaths had been needed to persuade the white chiefs in Washington to send his people back to the West. Of the 418 Nez Perces who had surrendered in 1877, only 268 were alive to make the journey back to Idaho in 1885.

As the Union Pacific train pulled into Idaho, Joseph looked out his window at hills greening to the spring sun.

"Almost home again," he said happily.

But all too soon he was faced with disappointment. His people were to be divided. They were given a choice between the Nez Perce Reservation at Lapwai and another smaller reservation near Colville, Washington. Chief Joseph was given no choice. He must go to Colville, the authorities said.

"Why?" he asked. "I want to stay in Idaho. It is near my Wallowa home."

"If you stay," the authorities told him, "you must stand trial for the Salmon River murders. Ranchers there plan revenge against you."

There was nothing understandable to Joseph in such unreasonable hatred. It was White Bird's three young men who had murdered, and all three were dead now, killed in the war.

He bowed his head in resignation. At least if he could not go back to the land of the Nez Perces, he had come home to high country. At least his wandering among strange hills was over.

He was more content when he saw that there were mountains on the Colville Reservation. Here with cold

177

water to drink and pure air to breathe, his people would not die of the evil malaria. Here the little children would grow fat and strong. Here the one hundred and fifty of his band who had chosen to remain with him might win back some of the wealth that once had made them a powerful people.

The weary chief pitched his lodge on the banks of the Nespelem River and slipped easily into the old, pleasant way of living.

"We are not free to roam where we will here," he told his people. "But we can ask and get permission to leave the reservation for hunting and fishing. There are deer and elk in the forests. The streams have plenty of trout and salmon. There are camas meadows and patches of wild berries for the women. We will be content here."

The government supplied his people with half-rations. Under their care the few horses allowed them soon increased into big herds. The cattle thrived.

"My people never will be as rich as they were in Wallowa," Joseph said to his old men. "But there is enough for all—food, clothing, warm lodges."

When the reservation agent built a small clap-boarded house for the chief, he scorned to live in it.

"I am happy in my lodge," he said. "I like my blazing fire and the smoky walls."

When the agency opened a school for children and

supplied a teacher, Chief Joseph often opened the door
and strode in to listen and watch. He smiled when he
saw the children drop their mischief at once to pay
flattering attention to the teacher. He knew that wary
black eyes watched for the brief smiles or the frown
of their chief, whose word was law for all the camp.
When the lessons were over, he stalked about the
schoolroom giving light punishment to the luckless
children who had not recited well.

One day a visiting white man showed the chief a
photograph of himself taken before the battles had
begun. Joseph studied the picture and shook his head
sadly.

"That man is dead," he said.

He knew that years of grief and exile had left deep-
graven lines of suffering on his face. He knew that he
was heavier now with age, although he was still broad-
shouldered and deep-chested. In the picture he wore
Indian garb; now he often wore white men's clothing,
although he still clung to the Indian way of wearing
his hair in braids. He hoped that he still had the same
grave dignity of bearing that the picture revealed. The
man in the picture was dead, but that man was still
chief. He had the respect of all the white men he met,
and the loyal love of his own people. It was enough.

In 1889, on a trip to Portland, Oregon, Chief Joseph
met again the man who had been his friend after the

surrender—Colonel C. E. S. Wood, who was then practicing law in Portland. The two friends talked over old times. Colonel Wood's eleven-year-old son begged to be introduced to the great chief. Joseph smiled, for he loved all children. Drawing the boy out with questions, he learned that Erskine was an excellent shot with the rifle and a skilled archer and fisherman.

"I go into the woods by myself," the boy said. "I camp and live on the game I shoot and on berries and fish."

"Like Nez Perce youths," Joseph said, smiling. Turning to the father, he suggested, "Let him visit my lodge in Nespelem. He will learn many things."

Two years later Erskine arrived at Joseph's camp. The boy was armed with his gun, bows and arrows, and fishing rod. Chief Joseph took the lad into his own lodge, turning him over to young Niky Mowitz, the chief's nephew and adopted son. Erskine was adopted into the tribe and given the name of Red Moon.

When he returned to Portland, he wrote his experiences in an article for *St. Nicholas Magazine.* His story, published in September, 1893, gives a picture of the life of Chief Joseph and his band on the Nespelem River. The boy wrote in part:

180

I helped the squaws cook some wild carrots once. . . . And Joseph said that I must not do squaw's work; that a brave man must hunt, fish, fight, and take care of the horses; but the squaws must put up the teepees, cook, sew, make moccasins and clothes, and take care of the household goods.

The boys take care of the horses. They catch them and drive them to and from the watering places; and the rest of the time they hunt with bows and arrows (the boys don't have guns) and fish and play games. . . .

The country is full of game, and we killed many a deer and a cinnamon bear. In the evening when they [the warriors] come home they talk about the day's hunt.

In 1897 Chief Joseph received an invitation to go to New York City to take part in the dedication of the tomb of Ulysses S. Grant. Joseph was to stay at the Astor House as the guest of that famous scout of Indian wars, Buffalo Bill Cody. Cody was at that time the owner of Buffalo Bill's Wild West Circus.

Chief Joseph was pleased to be so honored. For the trip he had a black broadcloth suit tailored, although he had been asked to bring with him his full ceremonial war dress.

"Will you wear your war bonnet of eagle feathers and your buckskin leggings and shirt while you are here?" the Astor House management asked him. "We want people to see the costume of a Nez Perce war chief."

Joseph smiled. "I will wear them. They are more comfortable than this white man's suit."

But the hotel guests came crowding around in rude curiosity. They wanted to see the "bloodthirsty savage" whose military skill had helped to hold off General Howard's soldiers through so many miles of wild country. Chief Joseph did not enjoy becoming a show, but he answered all their questions with unfailing courtesy, dignity, and a sharp sense of humor.

"Did you ever scalp anybody?" asked one woman.

Chief Joseph looked at her gravely and then smiled. She wore a big hat crowned with flowers and the wings of birds. Amused, he turned to his interpreter.

"Tell her," the chief said, pointing to the hat, "that I have nothing in my collection as fine as that."

Reporters begged for interviews, and he granted them in a kindly manner. In one of these talks he said:

> This East is strange to me. I do not understand it at all. The green of the trees and the grass is not here. The quiet of the woods is missing. It is all dirt and noise and hurry and the people are strange. . . . The white men have put up buildings you cannot see the top of. . . . They send the cars along on a rope [streetcars] . . . and they go up and down in the buildings without moving themselves

[elevators]. . . . Here in New York it is all wonders, and I do not understand how the people live. . . . It is good for me to see these things before I die.

Magnificent in full war regalia, Chief Joseph rode beside his old friend General Miles and Buffalo Bill in the parade. They rode to a ceremony honoring the President who had once signed the edict opening Wallowa to white settlement. But while the tomb of Grant was dedicated, Chief Joseph stood without bitterness or hate in his heart. The white chief was dead. Let the dead rest in peace.

But after the ceremony Joseph returned to the Astor House and packed his belongings. He could not abide the city any longer.

"I want to go where I can see some trees," he told the desk clerk.

Back in Nespelem the old chief felt more comfortable. Finer than the Astor House to him was his lodge, clean and tidy, with its Indian mats covering the packed dirt floor and his buffalo sleeping mats rolled at the sides. Here in Nespelem he was chief, not some queer animal for white people to stare at in curiosity.

17. THE LAST LODGE FIRE

WHEN he was sixty years old, Chief Joseph was granted the wish of his heart—to see Wallowa once more. He was an old man now, but he held himself proudly erect as he rode the hills and valleys of his home land. He found his father's grave and wept tears of joy when he saw that instead of being dishonored, it had been enclosed by a fence in the middle of a plowed field. Some white rancher had been kind.

Everywhere Joseph rode he saw rich meadows and plowed fields kept green by water from irrigation streams. He saw the fences and orchards and homes of the white men who now claimed his acres.

"By right of ancient tribal ownership," he told his companion, "these still are my acres. I have never sold this land."

185

Memories visited his shaking heart. Memories of white teepees by the bend of the shining river. Of the triumphant joy of a boy galloping his horse wild and free over sage-covered hills. Of the warm eagerness of the youth who had climbed above the blue lake to win a name powerful and proud.

Thunder-Rolling-in-the-Mountains—it was a name that stood for all power. Sadly he told himself that his *wyakin* had brought the man unharmed through many battles, but it had been powerless to give him the strength to lead his people back to their homeland. His mind told him that he would never live in the Valley of the Winding Waters again.

Back he rode to Nespelem to think and brood by his lodge fire. But he did not brood long. Knowing that effort was useless, he determined to continue the fight for Wallowa. Most of his life, he thought, had been a battle of words. He had talked words of logic to save Wallowa for his people and words of peace to keep them from bloodshed. Now with words he would still fight for the right of his people to live free in their own homeland. He would fight until he died.

Again he traveled to the East, this time to Washington, D.C., to ask President Theodore Roosevelt for a small piece of Wallowa. Chief Joseph was entertained in the White House, but his petition was not granted. Discouraged, he returned to Nespelem.

The Last Lodge Fire

In 1904 he again left his home. He had been invited to attend the commencement exercises of the Carlisle Indian Industrial School in Pennsylvania. He was surprised to find General Howard there—his old enemy. Chief Joseph was invited to attend a banquet and asked to speak. With grim humor, but with generosity, he said what was in his heart:

> Friends, I meet here my friend, General Howard. I used to be anxious to meet him. I wanted to kill him in war. Today I am glad to meet him. . . . We are both old men, still we live, and I am glad.

Then Chief Joseph went on to say words that showed his broad thinking and shrewd logic:

> I understand and I know that the learning of books is a nice thing, and I have some children here in school from my tribe. . . . I wish my children to learn more and more every day so they can mingle with the white people and do business with them.

In September of that year he made his last effort to win back Wallowa. White friends in Seattle had invited him to go there and present his case. He was a little fearful when he found that he was to speak in the largest auditorium in the city.

187

Thunder Rolling

"It would shake any Indian's heart," he told his interpreter, "to see a house so full of white people."

But when he began his talk through his interpreter, his voice gained in power as it rose and fell in the melodious, chanting tones of his own beautiful Nez Perce language. In his heart he felt that all talk was useless, but he would do what he could for his people.

The next day at the University of Washington he watched a football game.

"This is almost as good as a fast horse race," he told his interpreter.

Every time the players piled up in what looked like a battle, he became so excited that he rose to his feet. When the pile untangled itself into players again, he sat back with a sigh of "A-aa, that is good."

He did not notice that the co-eds and their escorts nearby were smiling at his broad hat and blanket, his two braids, and his excitement. He was too busy watching the white man's game.

Back to Nespelem in that early September of 1904 rode Chief Joseph, watching in silence from his seat beside the stage driver all the bright golden coloring of the quaking aspen on the hillsides and the scarlet flame of the sumac along the creek banks.

"I shall see another winter," he said to the stage driver.

But the great chief did not see another winter. In

188

The Last Lodge Fire

Nespelem he sat again by his lodge fire, seeing in the flames all the bright memories of his youth, all the bitter memories of battle in the swirling snow, the crushing memory of defeat and surrender.

As the September sun swung low, Chief Joseph surrendered to another and greater general than any of those he had fought. Out of the flames his old friends came to greet him, and he joined hands with them and went away to see the Great Spirit Chief.

A warrior paced a black horse slowly through the village on the banks of the Nespelem.

"Now Hin-mah-too-yah-lat-kekt sleeps!" he proclaimed. "Thunder-Rolling-in-the-Mountains sleeps."

For two days the great chief, dressed in his finest war robes, lay in state. His bear-claw necklace was clasped about his powerful neck. The ceremonial war bonnet adorned his head.

His friends, warriors who had fought in battle beside him, came to bid him good-bye. Little children who had loved him brought scarlet leaves from the hills or bright pebbles from the swift river—their farewell to their chief. When all who loved him had said good-bye, Chief Joseph was given back to his Mother Earth.

Many years have gone by since that September day, but the Wallowa Nez Perces still live on the banks of the Nespelem. Nez Perce boys and girl attend American universities and colleges. Nez Perce boys fought beside their white brothers in two World Wars. Nez Perce boys will fight as often as need be for the freedom of oppressed peoples, remembering a chief who loved freedom above all else. They will never forget a chief who in a few simple words expressed the age-long desire of mankind.

Let me be a free man, free to travel, free to stop, free to trade where I choose, free to follow the religion of my fathers, free to think and talk and act for myself—and I will obey every law or submit to the penalty.

CPSIA information can be obtained at www.ICGtesting.com
Printed in the USA
LVOW101311010313

322218LV00003B/542/P

9 781258 161866